You Are Not Your Brain

Why AI Can't Be Conscious and What That Reveals About Life After Death

by

Stephen Hawley Martin

The Oaklea Press

CONTENTS

"There are more things in heaven and earth, Horatio,
Than are dreamt of in your philosophy."

Shakespeare's Hamlet

Prologue: A Puzzle That Should Not Exist

On a winter evening in Seattle, a young woman named Maria was rushed into Harborview Medical Center. She had suffered a massive heart attack and by the time she arrived, her heart had stopped.

Doctors and nurses worked frantically to revive her. For several minutes Maria was clinically dead. Eventually, thankfully, the medical team succeeded in restarting her heart.

When she regained consciousness, she told the hospital staff something extraordinary. She said that while doctors were trying to save her life, she had been floating near the ceiling of the emergency room, and from that vantage point, she had watched the doctors working on her body below.

Experiences like this are often reported by people who come close to death. Many describe sensations of leaving their bodies and observing events from somewhere high up in the room, but Maria's story did not stop there. She said she had drifted outside the building. From there she noticed something unusual on a narrow ledge beneath a third-floor window: a single tennis shoe, which she described in detail.

The shoe, she said, was dark blue. One of the laces was caught beneath the heel. The toe area had been worn through.

A hospital social worker listened politely but remained skeptical. The story sounded implausible, but curiosity got the better of her. So she went outside to check.

After searching along the side of the building, she finally spotted it exactly where Maria had said it was—a single tennis shoe on the narrow ledge. It was dark blue. One lace was caught beneath the heel. The toe area was worn through.

The ledge could not be seen from inside the emergency room where Maria had been treated. Nor could Maria have noticed the shoe before arriving at the hospital. She had been unconscious when she was brought into the building.

Yet somehow she knew it was there.

When most people encounter stories like this, they assume there must be a simple explanation, or perhaps the story had been exaggerated. Maybe Maria had glimpsed the shoe earlier without realizing it. Maybe someone in the hospital had mentioned it in conversation. However, because I'd had a brief near death experience [NDE] at the age of 25, it didn't seem all that incredible to me. When mine happened, I also looked down at my body from up near the ceiling. Not only that, when I heard about Maria's NDE I was already aware that there are thousands of stories that prompt questions concerning the standard view that consciousness is created by and contained within the brain. Some involve patients who accurately describe medical procedures performed while they were clinically dead. Others involve children who appear to remember details of previous lives. Still others involved carefully controlled laboratory experiments suggesting that thoughts could influence physical systems in ways conventional science cannot explain.

Curiosity has a way of leading a person down unexpected paths, and frankly, I was curious—very curious, no doubt because my NDE had caused me to seriously doubt what I'd been taught in science classes in school and college—that my brain creates my consciousness. After it happened, I began reading the research of physicists, neuroscientists, psychologists, and the musings of philosophers. Over the course of three years, I personally interviewed more than a hundred scientists and others looking into the true nature of reality—quantum physicists, near death survivors, remote viewers who had used their abilities for the U.S. government to spy on Eastern Bloc adversaries, and half a dozen scientists working at the Division of Perceptual Studies [DOPS] at the University of Virginia School of Medicine. Many were asking questions that seemed heretical within the framework and the tenets of modern science:

What if consciousness is not produced by the brain?

What if consciousness is fundamental to the universe itself?

For more than three centuries, science has operated under a powerful assumption: that consciousness arises from the activity of the brain. According to this view, thoughts, awareness, and identity are nothing more than electrical and chemical activity among billions of neurons inside the skull. When the brain stops functioning, consciousness disappears.

Stories like Maria's, however, raise a troubling question:

If the brain truly creates consciousness, how could anyone observe events when the brain is no longer functioning?

As mentioned above, cases like this have now been reported thousands of times around the world. People whose hearts have stopped—whose brains should not be capable of producing conscious awareness—describe events that later prove to be accurate. Sometimes they report conversations that occurred in other rooms. Sometimes they describe objects or events later confirmed by medical staff.

Such reports present modern science with a puzzle it has not yet solved.

Suppose the prevailing assumption is wrong. Suppose consciousness does not originate in the brain at all. What if the brain is not the source of awareness but something more like a receiver—an instrument through which consciousness interacts with the physical world? If so, perhaps the physical world is not all there is. If that turns out to be true, the implications would be enormous. It would mean the most basic assumption underlying modern science—the belief that matter is primary and consciousness secondary—may be incomplete or incorrect. It would also mean our widely accepted beliefs about who we are, why we are here, and even what the universe itself is made of would have to change.

This book explores these possibilities. It follows a trail of evidence drawn from physics, neuroscience, philosophy, and carefully documented human experience. Taken together, these clues point toward a startling possibility:

Consciousness may not be a product of the universe.
It may be the foundation of it.

If that is true, the answer to the deepest human questions—Who are we? Why are we here? What is the nature of reality?—may be very different from what we have been taught to believe.

This investigation begins with a simple but profound question:

What if consciousness is fundamental?

Chapter One: Today's Dominant Worldview

For more than three centuries science has operated under a powerful assumption: that consciousness is produced by the brain. According to this view, thoughts, feelings, and awareness arise from electrical activity among billions of neurons. When the brain stops functioning, consciousness disappears.

Yet a growing body of evidence—from neuroscience, physics, and carefully documented human experience—suggests that this assumption may be incomplete. Increasingly, scientists are confronting a possibility once considered unthinkable: that consciousness may not be produced by matter at all.

If consciousness is fundamental rather than derivative, the implications are enormous. It would mean that the universe is far stranger than we imagined—and that understanding who we are and why we are here may require rethinking the very nature of reality.

Before examining evidence suggesting that consciousness may exist independently of the brain, however, it is important to understand how the opposite belief became so firmly established because the idea that the mind is produced by the brain seems obvious to most people today. It is taught in schools, assumed in medicine, and embedded in modern culture.

Nevertheless, this assumption is relatively new.

For most of human history, people believed that mind and consciousness were fundamental aspects of reality. Only in the past few centuries did the scientific worldview begin to shift toward the idea that the universe is comparable to a machine and nothing more than matter and energy operating according to mechanical laws. This view did not come about overnight. It unfolded gradually through a series of scientific discoveries that transformed humanity's picture of the cosmos. Understanding how that transformation occurred will help us understand why the prevailing worldview of today—what philosophers call "scientific materialism," also known as "physicalism"—became so dominant. It will also help explain why a growing number of scientists and researchers now believe that worldview may be incomplete.

To see how we arrived at our current understanding of reality, we must first look back at the intellectual revolution that reshaped science beginning in the seventeenth century. Only then can we begin to appreciate why new discoveries in physics, biology, and consciousness research are once again forcing us to reconsider the most fundamental questions of all:

What is the true nature of reality?

Who and what, in that reality, are we and why are we here?

Whether we realize it or not, we each have a worldview—a model in our minds of how things work. You might think of this as a stack of cans that forms a pyramid you might see as a grocery store aisle-end display. Each can represents an individual belief. Each belief in the display supports other beliefs. Change a foundational belief, and the whole thing might come tumbling down.

In the past hundred years or so, it seems to me that scientists have been presented with information that ought to have caused them to tear down the scientific materialist view of reality most of them still cling to and rebuild it from the ground up. Rather than do so, however, it appears that most of them have taken the easy way by dismissing as anomalies information that does not fit what they believe. If enough of these so-called anomalies build up, I suspect they will be like water backing up behind a dam. Unless scientists can explain how the phenomena described in this book can happen, given the scientific materialist paradigm, it is only a matter of time before that dam is going to burst. So that you will understand what I mean, let's take a look at how we got to the worldview, or model of reality, that eventually will be washed downstream.

There was a time, anthropologists tell us, when humans felt at one with nature. This can still be seen today in primitive cultures. Called pantheism, humans felt they were an integral part of the ecosystem. The Divine showed itself in many forms and was present in all things.

But as humans grew more self aware, they began to feel separation. The myth of Adam and Eve recalls the time when humans parted company with the view that they could commune with the Divine. They cut the cord by exercising free will.

No longer seeing God in themselves and in others, we humans conjured up gods outside ourselves. In ancient Greece, for example, many gods representing various human qualities were thought to exist. The worldview that evolved in those ancient times had man in the middle between two worlds—a place the Chinese referred to as the Middle Kingdom. The gods lived above the clouds of Mt. Olympus, although they did come to earth now and then, mostly to cause problems for humans.

Below the Middle Kingdom—what caused it to be in the middle—was the underworld, home of the dead, where Hades was in charge and the three-headed dog Cerberus guarded a gate one got to after crossing the River Styx.

Different cultures had different takes on this three-layered universe. Then as now, ideas about God and gods differed depending on the group one belonged to. The Egyptians had Bal. The Jews had Yahweh. The Romans and the Greeks had a pantheon full.

Then came Jesus of Nazareth and the idea emerged that only one God ruled over creation—although He did have angels and eventually saints who took up some of the positions left vacant by departing Roman and Greek gods. This God tended to be anthropomorphic—a man with a long white beard—as can be seen in Michelangelo's painting on the ceiling of the Sistine chapel.

In 1994 Karen Armstrong published a book, *A History of God,* which chronicled the history of the emergence of the concept of one God. Because of this idea, the worldview changed somewhat. God and angels replaced the pantheon of gods above the clouds. A fallen angel, Satan, replaced Hades. The place below the ground became hell rather than the underworld—where evildoers went. The good folk would be raised at the end of time on judgment day and given new, light bodies.

This view held sway for better than a thousand years but was destined to change again because of a new scientific discovery by Christopher Columbus (1451-1506).

Columbus lived on high ground overlooking a Mediterranean harbor. I have visited the ruin of what is said to be the house where he grew up. In that part of the world there is almost no humidity and the air is very clear. If Columbus had good eyes, he would not even have needed a spyglass to see ships climb up over the horizon as they approached the harbor. I've witnessed this myself. Columbus could see the world was round and he must have decided to prove it by sailing west to get to the spice islands of the East Indies.

Columbus apparently never realized it, but he didn't actually get there. Nevertheless, some of Ferdinand Magellan's (1480-1521) crew did, and beyond. Of the 237 men who set out on five ships in 1519, 18 actually completed the circumnavigation of the globe and returned to Spain in 1522.

The newly realized fact that the world was round forced the then commonly held worldview to change. Nevertheless, since people and, most important, Church leaders believed that God had created it, the earth remained at the center of the universe. Now heaven, the dwelling place of God, was seen as being somewhere above the stars. Hell was still beneath the ground, down where it was hot, the place from which molten lava spewed when volcanoes erupted.

It wasn't long before this worldview had to be updated. A fellow named Nicolaus Copernicus (1473–1543) determined the sun was at the center of the solar system. But the Church—the authority back then as science is today—pretty much ignored this concept because it did not go along with accepted canon.

A century later, along came Galileo Galilei (1564–1642), a man who would not leave well enough alone. Galileo—among other things an astronomer—championed Copernicus's assertion as proven fact. As a result, Galileo started having to watch his back. This was heresy. At that time people were being burned at the stake for less. Indeed, the leaders of the Church told Galileo he'd better recant, and he did. As a result, Galileo got off easy, spending the final years of his life under house arrest on orders of the Inquisition.

But even the Church couldn't keep word from getting out. Gradually, the accepted views of the day began to change.

In 1675, a Dutchman named Antoni van Leeuwenhoek (1632-1723) —an amateur lens grinder and microscope builder—saw for the first time tiny organisms he called "animalcules" living in stagnant water. He also spotted them in scum collected from his teeth. Leeuwenhoek didn't know or even speculate that "animalcules" might cause disease. It took until the late nineteenth century and Louis and Marie Pasteur for that revelation to dawn. At the time, the idea that creatures so small they were invisible to the naked eye entered the body to make a person sick and sometimes die would have seemed totally absurd. It was thought demons and the devil caused such things, or that God did it to punish sinners. In 1692 Salem, for example, 18 were hanged and one was crushed to death because they were thought to be witches in league with Satan. No wonder after that, and down until today, the idea of Satan and demons and witchcraft was thought to be pure superstition. To believe in such things was to invite witch-hunts and mass hysteria, and nobody wanted that.

Even so, a new day was dawning, a period alternately referred to as "The Age of Enlightenment" and "The Age of Reason." An English philosopher, Thomas Hobbes (1588-1679), had argued that aside from God—the "first cause" who created the material world—nothing existed that is not of the material world. The logic he used was simple. How could it be if God created everything?

This view was ultimately to lead to the great clock maker theory, the idea that God created the universe, wound it up, let it go, and was no longer involved in its operation. Natural laws also had been created that kept what had been set in motion going. Called Deism, many founding fathers, including Thomas Jefferson, subscribed to this view.

Hobbes had a big impact on the Age of Enlightenment, which was to pick up steam in the eighteenth century. But the big kahuna was Sir Isaac Newton (1643 – 1727), an English physicist, mathematician, astronomer, natural philosopher, alchemist, and theologian. Certainly one of the most influential men of all time, his *Philosophiæ Naturalis Principia Mathematica,* published in 1687, is considered to be the groundwork for most of classical mechanics. Newton described universal gravitation and the three laws of motion that dominated the scientific view of the physical universe at least until the advent of quantum mechanics. It seems safe to say Thomas Hobbes's materialistic view of reality coupled with Newton's mechanistic view is the bedrock of scientific thinking today, except perhaps among quantum physicists.

The prevailing worldview that emerged from the Age of Reason was that the universe might be compared to a giant machine. The Sun was at the center of the solar system. The Earth and planets revolved around it. Nothing existed but the material world. What was thought of in the seventeenth century and earlier as the invisible world of spirit did not exist. Everything that happened had a logical cause. Natural laws governed everything.

In 1859 an Englishman, Charles Darwin, published *On the Origin of Species*, a seminal work in scientific literature and a landmark work in evolutionary biology. Its full title, *On the Origin of Species by Means of Natural Selection, or the Preservation of Favoured Races in the Struggle for Life,* uses the term "races" to mean biological varieties. Darwin's book introduced the theory that populations evolve over the course of generations through a process of natural selection. It presented a body of evidence indicating the diversity of life arose through a branching pattern of evolution and common descent. In other words, God had not created the variety of life on the planet, nor had He created humans. All this had happened through a natural—what might be seen as mechanical—process. This became accepted as fact among the educated classes.

But astute scientists then and now realized something important was missing from Darwin's theory. It cannot be reconciled with the second law of thermodynamics, or the Law of Entropy—the fact that in a closed system things tend to break down and fall apart, rather than get better. In other words, your old car is not going to get better all by itself. It's going to require outside help, meaning you are going to have to write a check or pull out a credit card.

How then could life get more complex by accident? What caused DNA and its complicated computer-code like structure that directs the manufacture of proteins? In an upcoming chapter we will take a look at just how complicated the mechanism is. On top of that, what caused eyes, kidneys, hearts, livers, ears, and all those complex systems to develop?

Nevertheless, Darwin's theories reinforced the rationalist idea that the so-called supernatural was a figment of human imagination and—not wanting to be burned at the stake—most scientists probably wanted to keep it safely buried. Life and its diversity were results of a natural process known as "survival of the fittest" coupled with the environment in which a particular species had evolved. Intelligence and mind had evolved as life had evolved and had reached its pinnacle in humans. Mind and intelligence were produced by an organ, the brain, which had resulted from this evolution. Thought was created by the brain and would later be envisioned as being a result of electrons jumping across synapses. It was contained within the skull. ESP was impossible and so was remote viewing and mediumship.

With this worldview, a wedge was inserted and hammered in between science, religion and any possibility of things so called supernatural or paranormal. Hobbes had said nothing existed but the physical. If this were so, where could God possibly reside? What about the heavenly hosts? Thought was contained within the skull so what possible good could prayer do?

A line was drawn. Educated men and women could not believe in God and prayer or angels or ghosts and demons, which were seen as figments of ignorance and superstition. Many may have had a yearning for God—as humans seem to for the spiritual—but could not rationalize His existence. All were forced to choose between religion and science, though many attempted to straddle the line—as they still do today.

Now, at the beginning of the second quarter of the twenty-first century, this worldview continues to be the only socially acceptable one in some circles. But there are signs it is beginning to crumble. Hundreds of thousands, perhaps millions, have shifted to a new worldview based on a new branch of science called quantum mechanics and the findings of scientific research that do not fit the materialist-reductionist mold.

Let's look at some of the pioneers who have not been afraid to speak out, as well as their ideas and discoveries that conflict with the prevailing nineteenth-twentieth century worldview. The following does not in any way represent an exhaustive list. My apologies to anyone who feels left out, and to anyone who thinks I have overlooked a key figure.

Matter = Energy

In 1905, Albert Einstein (1879-1955), a German-born theoretical physicist, published a paper proving that light behaves both as a wave and as particles. This, as well as Einstein's famous formula, $E = MC^2$, indicates reality and matter are not what they seem. Matter or mass as it is referred to in this formula is equivalent to energy and vice versa.

In 1912 Swiss psychiatrist Carl Jung (1875-1961) published *Wandlungen und Symbole der Libido* (known in English as *The Psychology of the Unconscious)* that postulated a collective unconscious, sometimes known as collective subconscious. According to Jung there is an unconscious mind shared by a society, a people, or all humanity, that is the product of ancestral experience and contains such concepts as the classic archetypes, science, religion, and morality.

Quantum physicists came along who expanded on Einstein's work. Niels Henrik David Bohr, a Danish physicist, made fundamental contributions to understanding atomic structure and quantum mechanics, for which he received the Nobel Prize in Physics in 1922. He is quoted as having said, "Everything we call real is made of things that cannot be regarded as real."

Nothing is really solid. Everything is energy—vibrations.

Ironically, the true nature of reality has been known by a few scientists for almost a hundred years. It was revealed succinctly by Max Planck, born 1858 and died 1947, in an article that ran in the British newspaper, *The Observer* on October 25, 1931. Even though Max Planck was a Nobel Prize-winning German physicist and the father of quantum theory, Scientific Materialists have ignored his words because they do not fit with what they believe. Planck was quoted in that article as having said, "I regard consciousness as fundamental. I regard matter as derivative from consciousness. We cannot get behind consciousness. Everything that we talk about, everything that we regard as existing, postulates consciousness."

In 1944 Max Planck also said, "As a man who has devoted his whole life to the most clear headed science, to the study of matter, I can tell you as a result of my research about the atoms, this much: There is no matter as such! All matter originates and exists only by virtue of a force which brings the particles of an atom to vibration and holds this most minute solar system of the atom together... We must assume behind this force the existence of a conscious and intelligent mind. This mind is the matrix of all matter."

Also in the early 1930s a man named J. B. (Joseph Banks) Rhine moved from Harvard University to Duke to set up a parapsychology laboratory. Rhine not only founded the parapsychology lab at Duke, he also founded the *Journal of Parapsychology* and the Foundation for Research on the Nature of Man. His double blind studies conducted largely between 1930 and 1960 established that ESP exists and is real. They also showed psycho kinesis—mind over matter—is real as well, at least to a small degree.

His findings were either scoffed at or ignored by the scientific community then as they continue to be today.

In 1953, Eugen Herrigel (1884-1955), a German philosopher who taught philosophy at Tohoku Imperial University in Sendai, Japan, from 1924-1929 published the book, *Zen and the Art of Archery.* This introduced Zen Buddhism to the West and the concept that "All Is One," i.e., everything is connected rather than made up of separate parts. How else could Zen masters shoot arrows while blindfolded and consistently hit the bull's-eyes of targets many yards away?

In 1966 a British philosopher named Alan Watts (1915-1973) published a book called *The Book: On the Taboo Against Knowing Who You Are* that went into detail about Buddhist thought. Known as an interpreter and popularizer of Asian philosophies for a Western audience, Watts wrote more than 25 books and numerous articles on subjects such as personal identity, the true nature of reality, higher consciousness and the meaning of life. His writings and ideas fueled a new movement which came to be known as the New Age.

A polygraph expert named Cleve Backster began research in 1966 that demonstrated living plants tune into the thoughts and intentions of humans as well as other aspects of their environments, thus indicating some sort of hidden mental connection between living things. His findings were ridiculed, but have since been confirmed by other researchers.

In 1978 a young man with a B.A., M.A., and Ph.D. from the University of Virginia and an M.D. from Georgia Medical School named Raymond Moody (born 1944) published a book called *Life After Life,* in which he detailed the experiences of people who had been clinically dead and resuscitated.

Also in 1978, a psychiatrist named M. Scott Peck (1936-2005) published a book that became a huge bestseller called, *The Road Less Travelled: A New Psychology Of Love, Traditional Values And Spiritual Growth.* Among other things, Peck's book dealt with the phenomenon of grace. He said grace was both common and to a certain extent, predictable. He also wrote that, "grace will remain unexplainable within the conceptual framework of conventional science and 'natural law' as we understand it." Grace is the unseen force that brings the best possible results out of unfortunate events and circumstances, i.e., "every cloud has a silver lining." In Peck's own words, "There is a force, the mechanism of which we do not fully understand, that seems to operate routinely in most people to protect and encourage their physical health even under the most adverse conditions." His book gives specific examples.

In 1979, Gary Zukav, a former Green Beret during the war in Vietnam, published a book called the *Dancing Wu Li Masters: An Overview of the New Physics.* Targeted for laymen, it explained the basics of quantum physics in everyday language, i.e., without the use of complicated mathematics. Zukav concluded that "the philosophical implication of quantum mechanics is that all of the things in our universe (including us) that appear to exist independently are actually parts of one all-encompassing organic pattern, and that no parts of that pattern are ever really separate from it or from each other."

Also in 1979, James Lovelock published a book called *Gaia: A New Look at Life on Earth* that explained his idea that life on earth functions as a single organism. In contrast to the conventional belief that living matter is passive in the face of threats to its existence, the book explored the hypothesis that the earth's living matter—air, ocean, and land surfaces—forms a complex system that has the capacity to keep the Earth a fit place for life. Since Gaia was first published, many of Jim Lovelock's predictions have come true.

In the mid 1980s a television series appeared on PBS called *The Power of Myth,* featuring author and Sarah Lawrence College Comparative Religion Professor, Joseph Campbell (1904-1987). These programs made an impact on a significant segment of the public and opened their eyes to the possibility of the existence of what might be termed "a spiritual dimension." This can be summed up using Campbell's own words, "Anyone who has had an experience of mystery knows there is a dimension of the universe that is not available to his senses."

In July, 1988, Dr. Randolph Byrd, a cardiologist, published an article in the *Southern Medical Journal* about the effects of prayer on cardiac patients. Over a ten-month period, he used a computer to assign 393 patients admitted to the coronary care unit at San

Francisco General Hospital either to a group that was prayed for by home prayer groups (192 patients), or to a group that was not prayed for (201). A double blind test, neither the patients, doctors, nor the nurses knew which group a patient was in.

The patients who were remembered in prayer had remarkably, and a statistically significant number of better experiences and outcomes than those who were not prayed for. Also, fewer prayed-for patients died, although the difference between groups in this case was not large enough to be considered statistically significant.

In 1994 Rupert Sheldrake, a British biochemist, published a book called *A New Science of Life.* Sheldrake offered evidence that what he called "morphogenetic fields" worked together with an animal or a human's genes to form and shape the embryos that develop in mothers' wombs, saying that it was illogical to think that genes could do the job alone since all they actually do is produce proteins. Sheldrake wrote that if they also determine the shapes and parts of a body it would be "rather like delivering the right materials to a building site at the right times and expecting a house to grow spontaneously."

In 1995, Raymond Chiao, a Hong Kong native and quantum physicist then teaching at the University of California at Berkeley, published a paper about a series of experiments. The paper, reported upon in a July 1995 issue of *Newsweek* magazine, said that what researchers knew or did not know about certain aspects of each experiment had a predictable determination on their outcomes. In other words, what was in the researchers' minds—i.e. thought—apparently determined the result. In the *Newsweek* article reporting on this, Nobel Prize winning physicist Richard Feynman was quoted as having said this is the "central mystery" of quantum mechanics, that something as intangible as knowledge—in this case, which slit a photon went through—changes something as concrete as a pattern on a screen.

As will be discussed, in 2001, F. Holmes Atwater published a book detailing how he set up and managed the Stargate Project, a secret United States Army unit established in 1977 at Fort Meade, Maryland—until his retirement from the Army in 1988. In other words, psychics were used to gather what turned out to be accurate and important intelligence on the Soviet Union and Soviet Bloc nations.

Also in 2001, a study published in the September issue of the *Journal of Reproductive Medicine* showed that prayer was able to double the success rate of in vitro fertilization procedures that lead to pregnancy. The findings revealed that a group of women who had people praying for them had a 50 percent pregnancy rate compared to a 26 percent rate in the group of women who did not have anyone praying for them. In the study—led by Rogerio Lobo, chairman of obstetrics and gynecology at Columbia University's College of Physicians & Surgeons—none of the women undergoing the IVF procedures knew about the prayers on their behalf. Nor did their doctors. In fact, the 199 women were in Cha General Hospital in Seoul, Korea, thousands of miles from those praying for them in the

U.S., Canada and Australia. This collaborates with other studies and quantum physics theory that distance is not a factor at the subatomic level of mind.

Studies similar to this have been and are being carried out by a consortium of scientists put together by Lynne McTaggart, author of the book published in 2002, *THE FIELD: The Quest for the Secret Force of the Universe*, and her 2008 release, *The INTENTION EXPERIMENT: Using Your Thoughts to Change Your Life* and the World. When I interviewed her in early 2008, she described some of these experiments and the terrific success she and her colleagues have had. She said several of these studies were already being prepared for publication.

In 2007, Stephen E. Braude, then a professor of philosophy at the University of Maryland Baltimore County, published *The Gold Leaf Lady and Other Parapsychological Investigations.* The book tells the story of Katie, a woman who demonstrated that mind can produce matter—in this case brass: 80% copper and 20% zinc with its huge implications for quantum physics and the origins of the physical universe. I report on this in detail in other books.

Also in 2008, Julie Beischel, Ph.D., published a peer-reviewed paper in *The Journal of Parapsychology* in which she concluded, " . . . certain mediums can report accurate and specific information about the deceased loved ones (termed "discarnates") of living people (termed "sitters") even without any prior knowledge about the sitters or the discarnates and in the complete absence of any sensory sitter feedback. Moreover, the information reported by these mediums cannot be explained as a result of fraud or 'cold reading' (a set of techniques in which visual and auditory cues from the sitter are used to fabricate 'accurate' readings) on the part of the mediums or bias on the part of the sitters."

In summary, we humans developed a mechanistic view of reality in the eighteenth and nineteenth centuries that more recent research reveals clearly contradicts. The truth was revealed by Einstein, Planck, and other quantum physicists. The foundation of reality is consciousness and it is created, as Max Planck said, by a conscious and intelligent mind that is the matrix of all matter. Nothing is solid, everything is vibrations. The universe is energy, the foundation of which is consciousness, i.e., mind,, as Max Planck said. The implications of this are huge, only a few of which will be covered in this book.

Chapter Two: A Flawed Premise

The fundamental principle of science as it is taught in schools today, i.e., Scientific Materialism, is that nothing exists except material substance: "matter," in a single word. If matter is all there is, however, consciousness and intelligence could not have existed until evolution produced a brain. But, as you are about to see, powerful evidence suggests otherwise.

In 1957 Francis Crick [1916-2004] discovered that the chemical subunits along the interior of the double helix of DNA function like alphabetic characters in a written language, or the digital characters such as the zeros and ones in a computer code. No doubt you've seen DNA code printouts. Crick realized they direct the construction of proteins and protein machines that all cells need to stay alive. In other words, it came to light that digital information directs the construction of the crucial components of living cells. Therefore, to explain the origin of life, one would have to explain how this complicated processing system came about.

How complicated is it? According to an article on the website of *BBC Science Focus Magazine,* the UK's leading science and technology monthly: "The DNA in your cells is packaged into 46 chromosomes in the nucleus. As well as being a naturally helical molecule, DNA is super-coiled using enzymes so that it takes up less space. If you stretched the DNA in one cell all the way out, it would be about two meters long and all the DNA in all your cells put together would be about twice the diameter of the Solar System."

How incredible is that? The strand of DNA in a single cell is six feet, six inches long. That's a lot of code when you consider that the size of the characters in the code is microscopic. Think of the enormous amount of information packed into it.

It should go without saying that whenever we see information, and we trace it back to its source, whether it's computer code, a paragraph in a book, or a computer program, there is always an intelligent input that accounts for that information. This indicates, of course, is that intelligence is behind the origin of life, and yet an ardent Scientific Materialist would argue that given infinite time, anything can occur—for example, that a room full of monkeys with typewriters would produce *War and Peace* or the complete works of Shakespeare with no typos, given enough time.

What argues against this is that the universe began with the Big Bang 13.8 billion years ago and the realization that the earth is only about 4.5 billion years old. Of course, it's true that some scientists argue against the theory that the universe had a beginning. They believe the universe has always existed and that it contracts and expands. But whether it had a beginning or has always existed and contracts and expands, the result would be the same—it got off to a (perhaps new, after an infinite number of previous) start(s) 13.8 billion years ago. This is indicated by a broad range of phenomena, including the abundance of light elements, the cosmic microwave background (CMB), large-scale structure and Hubble's law, i.e., the farther away galaxies are, the faster they are moving away from Earth.

According to calculations made by mathematicians who are a lot smarter when it comes to arithmetic than I am, the odds are much too long for life to have happened by accident, given that the earth is only 4.5 billion years old and life began on earth 3.77 years ago. That leaves 730 million years for the monkeys to have typed out six feet, six inches of microscopic code—with no typos.

I can almost hear someone reading this book thinking: "Yeah, well, maybe life was brought here by a space alien." Maybe. But where did he or she get it? And who or what created the space alien?

It seems to me that anyone who thinks deeply about what is written above would have to come to the conclusion that information resembling computer code that directs something complicated to happen must be the product of some sort of intelligence. And yet that would have been impossible if material substance—matter—is all there is because, to repeat what was just stated, if that were the case, intelligence could not have existed until evolution produced a brain.

Not every scientist has turned a blind eye to the facts. After Click's discovery, a number of them began to see that there must be some sort of guiding intelligence responsible for the origin of life. I know this from personal experience because I read a book more than forty years ago that put forth that argument. Published in 1975, it refuted the idea that intelligence, consciousness, and awareness, came about as a result of evolution. The book was entitled *Intelligence Came First.* It was produced by a group of well qualified individuals that met monthly to read and discuss material that was compiled and edited by Ernest Lester Smith [1904-1992], a Fellow of the Royal Society—the prestigious scientific academy of the United Kingdom, dedicated to promoting excellence in science.

Intelligence Came First caused quite a bit of controversy when it came out. Among other things, the book put forth the DNA, computer code argument above, and it also noted that throughout the eons of evolution, needs have preceded the organs through which they are fulfilled—eyes, ears, taste buds, hearts, kidneys, and so forth. Since each new organ developed in response to a need, the book's contributors argued, why would the brain be an exception? The conclusion the book's authors and contributors came to was that intelligence came first, quite able to function in its own realm.

I still have a copy of this book, which has long been forgotten perhaps by everyone except me—because Materialists shouted it down with a vengeance. But think of the intelligence that would be required to design any one of those organs. Could all of them have come about by chance, i.e., random mutations followed by natural selection? Who that's really thought about the complexity of an eye, a liver, or a kidney could possibly think it could have happened by accident? And yet it appears that back in 1975, the scientific community did just that, and apparently many still think that way today.

In 2007, many years after reading that book, I took the opportunity to become the talk show host and producer of a podcast called *The Truth about Life.* For three years I read, and over that period of time interviewed, more than a hundred authors engaged in quests for truth. Among them were medical doctors, parapsychologists, metaphysicians, physicists specializing in quantum mechanics, near death survivors, theologians, psychiatrists, psychologists, and all manner of researchers into the true nature of reality. I don't recall any of these cutting-edge individuals who actually held to a Materialist point of view, except one guest who could not produce any facts to back up his claims. All he could come up with was something to the effect that a particular claim "cannot be so because it goes against what science tells us."

What does materialist science tell us? Darwin's theory is that mutations happen randomly and that those that help an organism survive long enough to reproduce are passed on to the next generation. That makes sense and is likely an important factor in how organisms adapt when their environments change, but how in the world would that lead to an eye, or an ear, or a kidney?

Suppose, for example, that a chance process does result in something that's moving in the right direction for the creation of a kidney—or to back up a bit, to the creation of computer-like code in DNA that makes life possible in the first place? Entropy, i.e., the natural direction of spontaneous change toward disorder, will work against making further progress. In other words, entropy will likely unwind that progress before additional progress can be made.

In summary, the chance-based argument is faulty for two reasons: 1) time works against the chemical synthesis of life, and 2) there is a limit to the amount of time for it to have happened. Using the example of a four-dial bike lock, for example, how likely is it that a thief will be able to break the four-digit code? The odds will be against it happening unless he has enough time to sample more than half of the possible combinations. Therefore, when assessing the plausibility of a random search for an informational sequence, it's necessary to assess how many opportunities there are to do so, versus the complexity of the sequence.

With respect to life, it turns out that when you do the math, both in the pre-biotic case (the conditions that make life possible) and in the biological case (once life exists, that mutation and selection result in the evolution of life), the complexity of the sequences is so great—making the number of combinations that would have to be searched so large that there is not enough time to have built standard length functional proteins, much less life itself.

Grok's Analysis

Have a look, for example, at what Elon Musk's powerful AI assistant, Grok 4, has to say about this. According to an article by Calvin Smith, a Canadian who is the Executive Director of Answers in Genesis:

- When asked about spontaneous abiogenesis (life arising from non-living chemistry) under strictly defined conditions (i.e., "use only logic, mathematical probability, and observational science; do *not* rely on ideology or consensus"), Grok estimated the probability of a minimal genome forming randomly as less than 1 in 10^200. That's a one in 10 followed by one heck of a lot of zeros.

- Regarding the probability of a new functional gene of ~1,000 nucleotides emerging purely by mutation and chance, Grok gave odds around 1 in 10^600. That's a one in 10 followed by more zeros than hardly anyone can count.

- Under those conditions, Grok concluded that unguided chemical evolution was "effectively impossible" within the time available on Earth (the standard scientific view is that it took 600 million years from when earth was formed until live appeared), and thus the most logical explanation was "a directed process implying a purposeful, intelligent design." In other words, an intelligent agent was the likely cause.

In other words, Grok 4 confirmed that Ernest Lester Smith and his colleagues were correct. Intelligence came first. It was necessary for life to come about and is what's behind the evolution of organisms. This is likely to be difficult to accept if not mindblowing for ardent Physicalists, but it is extremely important for the rest of us because it is important evidence in the search for understanding who and what humans are and why we are here.

Chapter Three: Artificial Intelligence and the Hard Problem

As I write these words in March 2026, a debate is going on in the media concerning whether or not artificial intelligence might someday become conscious. The assertion that it could is based upon an assumption: that consciousness emerges automatically from sufficiently complex information processing. If true, the story seems straightforward. Life evolved increasingly sophisticated nervous systems. Eventually the human brain appeared—an organ containing roughly eighty-six billion neurons connected by trillions of synapses. Humans then built computers that process information electronically. Today those systems can recognize speech, write essays, compose music, and defeat human champions in complex games like chess. If intelligence arises from computation, the argument goes, perhaps consciousness will eventually arise from sufficiently advanced computation as well.

The problem with this reasoning, however, is that it quietly assumes something that has never actually been demonstrated: that computation produces experience. In fact, nothing at all in the mathematics of computation requires experience to exist.

The Hard Problem of Consciousness

In the 1990s philosopher David Chalmers gave a name to the central mystery of mind: "The Hard Problem of Consciousness."

Science can explain many aspects of cognition. Neuroscience can map the circuits involved in perception, memory, and decision-making. Researchers can even predict which brain regions will activate when a person sees a face or hears a melody.

These are what Chalmers called the "easy problems."

They explain how the brain processes information, but they do not explain why those processes are accompanied by subjective experience.

Why, for example, should electrical activity in the visual cortex produce the experience of seeing the color red? Why does neural activity in the auditory cortex produce the sensation of music? Why is there an inner world of experience at all?

A Thought Experiment

To illustrate this problem, philosopher Frank Jackson proposed a thought experiment that has become famous in the philosophy of mind. Imagine a scientist named Mary is the world's leading expert on color vision. She knows everything that physics, neuroscience, and biology can tell us about how color perception works.

She understands the wavelengths of light. She understands how the retina converts light into neural signals. She understands how the brain processes those signals.

There is only one unusual feature of Mary's life. She has lived her entire life in a black-and-white environment. Her room is black and white. Her books are black and white. Even the screens she studies display only shades of gray. Mary knows everything science can say about color, but she has never seen it.

Now imagine that one day Mary steps outside her monochrome room and sees a red rose for the first time. At that moment, something remarkable happens. Mary learns something new. She learns what red actually looks like and how that makes her feel.

This thought experiment raises an extraordinary question. Before leaving the room, Mary already knew all the physical facts about color vision. If physical knowledge were complete, she should have known everything there was to know about seeing red. Yet when she actually experiences red, she learns something new. She gains knowledge that cannot be captured in physical descriptions alone. This suggests a startling conclusion:

There are facts about consciousness that cannot be reduced to physical facts.

In other words, subjective experience contains something that physical science does not fully explain.

Why This Matters

This conclusion strikes at the heart of the materialist view of mind.If consciousness were entirely produced by physical processes, then a complete physical description of those processes should contain everything there is to know about experience.

Mary's discovery shows that this cannot be the case.

Knowing every physical detail about the brain does not automatically reveal what an experience feels like. The experience itself contains something additional—something that exists only from the inside.

What Neuroscience Actually Shows

When neuroscientists study the brain, they observe correlations between neural activity and conscious states. Certain patterns of brain activity accompany particular experiences. Damage to specific regions of the brain can alter perception or memory, but correlation does not prove causation. A radio's circuitry, for example, correlates with the music you hear, yet the radio does not produce the broadcast signal. Likewise, the presence of neural activity associated with a conscious experience does not demonstrate that the activity creates the experience.

It only shows that the two occur together.

Several lines of research increasingly suggest that the brain may function less like a generator of consciousness and more like a system that shapes or channels it.

The Psychedelic Paradox

One intriguing clue comes from research on psychedelic substances such as psilocybin and LSD. Brain-imaging studies consistently show something unexpected during intense psychedelic experiences—experiences many participants describe as profoundly vivid and expansive—activity in certain organizing regions of the brain actually decreases. In particular, activity in the default mode network, which normally helps maintain the brain's narrative sense of self, becomes significantly quieter.

If the brain were producing consciousness the way a computer produces output, reducing activity should reduce experience. Yet subjects frequently report the opposite: expanded awareness, heightened perception, and profound emotional insight. Instead of consciousness fading as neural control diminishes, it sometimes appears to broaden. This finding is difficult to reconcile with the idea that the brain manufactures consciousness. It fits more comfortably with the idea that the brain may normally filter or constrain a broader field of consciousness.

A Remarkable Incident at UVa

An incident similar to the one recounted in the Prologue occurred at the University of Virginia. It happened early in the medical career of psychiatrist Dr. Bruce Greyson, and it had the effect of directing his attention to near-death experiences. Dr. Greyson was treating a woman who had attempted suicide and had been admitted to the hospital in a deeply unconscious state. For hours she remained completely unresponsive.

The following day, after regaining consciousness, she told him something that didn't make sense to him. While unconscious, she said, she had found herself looking down at the hospital room from a vantage point near the ceiling. From that perspective she could see the medical team working below. Then she mentioned something very specific. She told him she had noticed a stain on his tie. Not only that—she described exactly where the stain was located.

Greyson looked down. There was indeed a stain on his tie, partially hidden beneath his lab coat and not easily visible from the patient's position in the hospital bed.

Experiences like this do not categorically prove that consciousness can exist independently of the brain, but they do raise a question neuroscience has yet to answer:

How can a patient who is deeply unconscious report accurate observations of events occurring around them?

Cases like these led Greyson to devote decades to studying near-death experiences, eventually documenting thousands of reports with striking similarities. In an upcoming chapter, you will read the conclusion he came to.

Why Computation Cannot Produce Experience

A powerful philosophical argument also suggests that consciousness cannot arise from computation alone. Computation is simply the manipulation of symbols according to rules. Computers process electrical states—ones and zeros—through mathematical operations, but the symbols themselves have no intrinsic meaning to the machine. For example, a computer can process the word *apple*. It can store it, transmit it, and use it in sentences. However, the machine does not experience the smell of an apple orchard or the taste of a ripe apple.

Even the most advanced AI systems operate through vast networks of mathematical pattern recognition. They manipulate symbols with extraordinary sophistication, but nowhere in the process is there a step that logically produces subjective awareness. This is why intelligence and consciousness must be carefully distinguished.

Intelligence processes information, whereas consciousness experiences reality. The two can coexist—but they are not the same thing.

Chapter Four: Consciousness and the Brain

In light of the facts covered so far, could it be possible that the brain doesn't actually create consciousness or store memories? What if it is actually a receiver that might be compared to a cell phone or radio—one that integrates consciousness and the body? We are about to look at evidence that indicates this may be the case. Wouldn't this suggest the possibility that some sort of primeval intelligence might exist that created life in the first place?

During the three-year period from 2007 through 2009, when I was the producer and host of a podcast called "The Truth About Life," I interviewed quite a number of scientists who were investigating this possibility. One mentioned earlier in Chapter One was Julie Beischel, the Director of Research at the Windbridge Research Center (See: https://www.windbridge.org/). Dr. Beischel has a Ph.D. in Pharmacology and Toxicology with a minor in Microbiology and Immunology. She uses her interdisciplinary training to apply the scientific method to controversial topics.

Dr. Beischel received her Ph.D. from the University of Arizona at a time when something occurred to prompt her to change the direction of her career away from pharmacology and to investigation of the paranormal. Her mother committed suicide. The death of a parent can be devastating—no doubt even more so when it happens by suicide—and Dr. Beischel wanted answers. I don't know what questions she might have had, but a basic one was likely, "Does my mother's consciousness still exist?" Dr. Beischel told me in our interview that science is her religion. Quite naturally, that's where she turned for the answer. She wanted to know what science could tell her about life after death.

"Very little," was what she found out.

As fate would have it, a good deal of what little research was being done on this subject was being conducted by Dr. Gary Schwartz at the University of Arizona—precisely where Dr. Beischel happened to be.

A book by Schwartz detailing his work with mediums was published in 2002 by Atria called, *THE AFTERLIFE EXPERIMENTS: Breakthrough Scientific Evidence of Life After Death.* Apparently, Dr. Schwartz had been subjected to a good deal of criticism from skeptics about this research. His critics claimed his methodologies were riddled with holes. Finding a spot for Dr. Beischel in his research laboratory no doubt made a lot of sense because she was trained to come up with methodologies no one could poke holes in. For the next couple of years she worked closely with him.

I asked Dr. Beischel about Dr. Schwartz's work, much of which had been done before she joined him. She wouldn't talk about that except to say when she came on board she felt more stringent controls were needed. In 2007 when Schwartz's research turned in a different direction, Dr. Beischel and her husband, Mark Boccuzzi—who'd been researching hauntings—founded the Windbridge Institute.

Dr. Beischel then developed a methodology that passed peer review scrutiny with flying colors to test the abilities of mediums that claim to communicate with the dead. At the time of our interview, Windbridge was granting certification to mediums that successfully completed the screening process. It involved an intensive eight-step procedure that took about a year:

Step 1: Written Questionnaire
Step 2: Personality/Psychological Tests
Step 3: Phone Interview (with an existing WCRM)
Step 4: Phone Interview (with a Windbridge Investigator)
Step 5: Two Blinded Phone Readings
Step 6: Mediumship Research Training
Step 7: Human Research Subjects Training
Step 8: Grief Training

Each medium that became certified was required to agree to donate a minimum of four hours per month to assist in various aspects of the research, to uphold a code of spiritual ethics, and to abide by specific Windbridge standards of conduct.

Before we discuss Dr. Beischel's mediumship research, let me define some terms. A "discarnate" is a dead person with whom a medium supposedly communicates. A "sitter" is the loved one of the discarnate for whom the reading is done. A "proxy sitter" is someone who asks the medium questions in place of the sitter. A proxy sitter must be someone that knows nothing about the discarnate.

The procedure was as follows. Two different, unrelated individuals (sitters) were selected that each wanted to contact a deceased loved one. Questions were developed for the discarnates of these sitters, including specifics such as a physical description, cause of death, and the discarnate's occupation or hobbies during life. The discarnates to be contacted in these paired sessions had to be of the same sex but have different physical descriptions, occupations in life, ages, and manners of death. This was done so that no confusion would be possible concerning which of the two discarnates was responding, assuming the answers given through the medium to the proxy sitter were correct.

Dates and times were set for the readings, usually on separate days.

Sitters were not told the times or dates of readings but were asked to request that the deceased loved one communicate with the medium at the designated time.

A proxy sitter that had no knowledge of a discarnate except for the first name contacted the medium by telephone at the prescribed date and time.

Let's say the discarnates are Suzie and Betty. The session asking the medium questions for Suzie would be recorded and then transcribed.

On the day and time of the next reading, the questions for Betty would be asked. This session was also recorded and transcribed. Ambiguous answers were adjusted so that they lacked ambiguity. For example, if the medium said Suzie's hair color was reddish, the answer was changed to "red."

Following these sessions, both sitters were given both sets of answers—without names on them. They were asked to score the answer to each question for accuracy and then rate each report on a scale of one to six based on how strongly each report portrayed the loved one (the discarnate) the sitter had hoped would be contacted.

This procedure eliminated the possibility of fraud. All the proxy sitter and the medium knew about a discarnate was his or her first name, making it impossible to find out anything about the deceased individual through conventional means. The medium could not give answers based on visual or verbal clues because the proxy sitter asking the medium questions knew nothing about the discarnate, and the session was conducted by telephone.

Rater bias also was eliminated. The sitter did not know which answer sheet was for his or her loved one and which was not. In addition, because the answers dealt in specifics—physical description, occupation, manner of death and so forth—ambiguity was eliminated, as was the tendency for wishful thinking on part of a sitter.

Dr. Beischel said that discarnates often found ingenious ways to communicate their presence and survival to a loved one. In one case, a discarnate communicated to the medium about a white car the medium had purchased on Halloween, which the medium had nicknamed "Casper"—for the friendly cartoon ghost. When asked why the discarnate might have done so, the sitter said, "Well, I suppose it's because our last name is Kasperi."

The results of this research were highly significant, statistically. On a scale of one to six—with one being not at all accurate, and six extremely accurate—the average score was about 3.5 for readings containing the loved one's answers, and less than 2.0 for the control readings, which is a sizable difference. These two scores are the averages of many compilations done over time. Some readings had much higher scores and some lower. Even the scores of readings in which the discarnate may have decided not to participate have been averaged in.

Dr. Beischel told me that after a research session was done, sitters would often contact the mediums directly for a follow up session, and that follow up sessions normally produced accuracy scores in the neighborhood of 85 to 90 percent.

The most obvious explanation for the findings of this research is that human consciousness continues after death. This is supported by research being conducted at the University of Virginia. It is also supported by the experiences of the mediums themselves. All consistently reported a difference between a session communicating with a discarnate, and what is called a psychic reading, which is done for a living person. They typically feel a presence when dealing with a discarnate.

Dr. Beischel is not the only scientist to conduct experiments to see if thought extends beyond the confines of the brain. As touched upon earlier, back in the early 1930s a university with a new name and big ambitions hired a couple of men who wanted to unravel the mysteries of the paranormal. That university was Duke, located in Durham, North Carolina, one of the most prestigious in the United States. The men were William McDougall and Joseph Banks Rhine, most often referred to as J. B. Rhine. The organization they created was called the Duke Parapsychology Laboratory for many years. Today it is called The Rhine Research Center, and although it is no longer connected with the University, it is located adjacent to the Duke campus.

What motivated these men? They wanted most to prove or disprove the fact or fiction of life after death. On my podcast that aired the week of April 6, 2009, I interviewed journalist Stacy Horn who wrote a book chronicling the history of this organization from 1930 to 1960, including experiments that were conducted and the interaction of the many people with the lab over the years. This included such well-known celebrities Upton Sinclair and scientists such as Albert Einstein. The name of her book is *UNBELIEVABLE: Investigations into Ghosts, Poltergeists, Telepathy, and Other Unseen Phenomena,* from the Duke Parapsychology Laboratory (HarperCollins, ECCO Imprint, 2009). Stacy went into this project a skeptic about paranormal phenomena, but was no longer a skeptic when she came out of it.

Previously known as Trinity College, a grant by tobacco millionaire James B. Duke in 1924 prompted the name change. Perhaps, the newly reconstituted school was looking for ways to make its mark when it lured William McDougall from Harvard University to set up a department of psychology.

He was soon contacted by a man named John Thomas who had 800 pages of transcripts generated by mediums he had been working with. Thomas' wife had died unexpectedly during an operation, and Thomas had been devastated. He began working with mediums in order to communicate with her.

Thomas got encouraging results, but he wasn't sure he could believe them. Looking for verification of their authenticity, he traveled around the United States talking with mediums. He went to Europe, eventually, reasoning that mediums there would have no way of knowing anything about him or his wife. If they were able to come up with information that was accurate, it would be more convincing.

Ultimately, Thomas wrote to McDougall asking if he could send J. B. Rhine, then of Harvard University, and Rhine's wife Louisa, to Duke to study this material. McDougall agreed and Rhine came to Duke.

Rhine studied Thomas' transcripts. He was able to verify much of the information, and to all but eliminate fraud and lucky guesses. He traveled to Upstate New York, for example, investigating cemetery head stones to check out the veracity of genealogy of Thomas' wife indicated by a medium. The genealogy proved to be accurate. Not even Thomas himself knew if this genealogy was correct, but the information did check out. Ultimately, however, Rhine concluded that even though the information was correct, it could not be said with absolute certainty that the information was coming from Thomas' deceased and now disembodied wife because there was no way to prove that what Rhine called "superpsi," and others label "the Akashic Records," wasn't the source of information tapped into by mediums who had supposedly been in touch with Thomas' wife. Superpsi or the Akashic Records is thought to be a psychic reservoir—a compendium of all human events, thoughts, emotions, and intent ever to have occurred located in what might be described as a nonphysical "cloud storage" facility. The compendium is supposed to be accessible by those with sensitive psychic abilities.

Rather than continuing to work with mediums, Rhine decided to put his energy into the study of what became known as extra sensory perception, or ESP. He reasoned that if he could prove awareness extends beyond, and exists outside the body, a major step would be taken toward establishing the possibility of survival of consciousness after death. After all, for our consciousness to continue after death it has to be capable of existing outside the body and the brain.

Rhine's most famous experiment used what has become known as ESP cards. Developed specifically for this purpose, these had different symbols on them including a star, wavy lines, a cross, a box and a circle. Many of these experiments were conducted—mostly using Duke University students—to see if people could tell what symbols were on the cards without looking at them. It was found again and again that they could.

The controls employed in these experiments were refined over time until neither the students nor those testing them could see one another. Ultimately, research was conducted in such a way that not even the person conducting the experiment knew what symbol was on the card a student was to identify. The experiments turned up statistically significant results time after time, showing that ESP is real.

One of Rhine's subjects in the ESP experiments was particularly impressive. A divinity student, his name was Hubert Pierce. Rhine believed that everyone possessed psychic abilities, but his research indicates some people have more talent for it than others. This is of course true of other abilities. An extremely talented singer will wow the judges and go on to win American Idol, but most will fail miserably and get the boot at the first audition.

There were twenty-five cards in the ESP deck, and five different symbols. Therefore, one would expect to guess five correctly each time through, simply by chance. Hubert Pierce could consistently get more than five correct, as could a number of others. But the interesting thing is, and according to Stacy Horn this came up frequently in the research, emotions played a role. Hubert, for example, needed money. He was a poor, struggling college student. Rhine once told him if he got the next card right, he'd pay him a hundred dollars. Pierce got it right. Rhine said, "Okay, get the next one right, and you'll get another hundred dollars."

Pierce got the next one right.

This went on through the entire deck. Pierce named all 25 cards correctly.

At one point, however, Hubert said he would not be coming into the lab for tests. His girlfriend had broken up with him, and he was heartbroken.

When he finally did come back, he did not perform well.

Another example of emotions playing a roll was the time Rhine tested the psychic abilities of children at an orphanage. One little girl became quite attached to a woman researcher. The little girl performed extremely well, apparently because she was eager to please, and wanted to prolong the session.

Something else that demonstrates awareness is nonlocal—at no particular place but everywhere at once—is the phenomenon of remote viewing. Those adept at remote viewing can direct their consciousness to be anywhere they want it to be. They use psychic powers to observe what's happening at a distant location—in terms of miles and in some cases, time as well.

Back in the 1970s, the U. S. government learned that the KGB was using psychics to spy on the United States. Naturally, U.S. Intelligence leaders wanted to see if this actually worked. U.S. Army Major General Edmund R. Thompson, who was deputy Director for the Management and Operations for Defense Intelligence from 1982-84 is quoted as having said, "I never liked to get into debates with the skeptics, because if you didn't believe that remote viewing was real, you hadn't done your homework."

It is apparently a fact that remote viewing was used beginning in the early 1970s and continuing throughout the Cold War to keep tabs on what the Soviets and Eastern Bloc countries were up to in locations that couldn't be observed by spy planes, satellites, or operatives on the ground. In the spring of 2009, I interviewed F. Holmes Atwater, who set up a U.S. Army Intelligence unit mentioned earlier called Stargate for the purpose of remote viewing. Atwater is known to friends as "Skip."

Skip got into this line of work through a series of what some people might call amazing coincidences, and others would say are synchronicities—events that look like coincidences, but happen for a reason. He grew up in a home with parents that took such things for granted. It was the sort of thing they talked about at the dinner table. As a kid, Skip told me he would go off on out-of-body trips almost nightly. Once, when he was seven or eight years old, it had to do with the problem he had with bedwetting.

"It was embarrassing," he said. "I had a big, brown piece of rubber on my bed so I wouldn't ruin the mattress. My parents didn't scold me, but they did make me wash my own sheets.

"I distinctly remember waking up one night, and I was all wet. I was screaming in anger, and my mother came in and said, 'What's wrong? Did you fall out of bed?'

"I said, 'No, I remember, I got up, and I went down the hall to the bathroom, and I sat down. And the minute I started to pee, I woke up here in bed, and I'm all wet.'

"I was mad as the dickens, and my mother hugged me and said, 'Oh, that's all right, don't worry about it. You know, Skip, sometimes you're in your body and sometimes you're out of your body, and you have to remember that when you're going to the bathroom, make sure you're in your body.'

"[What she said] made perfect sense to me, and I said, 'Oh, now I understand,' and that was the end of my bedwetting."

Skip was in the Army working for Army Intelligence when he came across a book called *Mind Reach* by Russell Targ and Harold E. Puthoff of the Stanford Research Institute. The book explained remote viewing, which didn't seem at all unusual to him, given his experiences as a child. It was as though a light had suddenly flicked on. He instantly realized this could be used to gather intelligence.

At the time, Skip was in counter intelligence. It was his job to defend against wiretaps, bugging devices, and other forms of intelligence gathering by the enemy. No one in his counter intelligence unit had thought about remote viewing as a way the enemy might be spying on us. So Skip went to his commanding officer, a Colonel Webb, and gave him the book. After the Colonel finished reading it, Skip asked him if this remote viewing was being used on our side.

The Colonel had no idea. He thought if anything were going on, the Pentagon would be the place to find out. So he had Skip transferred to the Pentagon to take a position where he'd be in charge of a counter intelligence team. Skip would have the access he needed to find out about remote viewing and what if anything was being done about it to prevent the enemy from using it.

Before Skip was able to relocate to Washington, however, he received a change of orders. He was told to report to Fort Meade in Maryland. This was a better location for a young Army officer with a wife and children, which Skip had, because Fort Meade had family housing and good schools. It would be a much more affordable and pleasant place to live than Washington, D.C.

At Fort Meade, Skip was assigned to what was known as a SAVE team—Security Activity Vulnerability Estimate team. The job was to go to sensitive U.S. installations and try to penetrate them in any way possible—as the enemy might in order to gather intelligence. Then the team would make a report to the commanding officer and provide recommendations for improving security.

Skip moved into his new job and was assigned an office that had just been vacated. The file cabinet and most of the desk drawers had been cleaned out, and an office safe had been emptied, but he did come across three documents in a bottom drawer of the desk that turned out to be classified. They reported on remote viewing experiments taking place in the Soviet sphere, funded by the KGB.

Skip took the documents to his supervising officer, a Major Keenan.

The Major looked at them. "Oh, yes, I remember these," he said. "The Lt. Colonel was very interested in this subject. Do you know anything about it?"

"Why, yes, I do, Major."

The Major took a moment and sized up Skip. "Lieutenant," he said, "from now on you're in charge of it."

And that's how Skip got his wish and began a ten year career that eventually put him in charge of a remote viewing unit of the Army.

Skip soon learned that basic research had been underway since 1972 to check the validity of the Eastern Bloc experiments. The initial question had been whether reports of success were valid. It could have been that the Soviets were falsifying the results in order to create fear. The Stanford Research Institute had been retained to replicate the KGB experiments, and to the surprise of the U.S. intelligence community, the results had been positive.

By the time Skip got involved, the CIA and other U.S. intelligence agencies had been using natural psychics for some time to gather information, including well-known psychics such as Ingo Swann, who has since written several books on remote viewing. Skip's job became to set up, recruit and train remote viewers for U.S. Army Intelligence who might or might not have had prior experience using their psychic abilities. He developed a screening process, and for those who made the cut, a training program employing methodologies gleaned from accomplished remote viewers.

Skip's efforts met with success, but after a while he began looking for ways to enhance the results that his remote viewers were achieving. This led him to The Monroe Institute (TMI) in Virginia, where he worked as Research Director when I interviewed him.

Robert Monroe (1915–1995) had spent a career in broadcasting, culminating as a vice president of NBC Radio. After leaving NBC, Monroe became known for his research into altered states of consciousness. His 1971 book *Journeys Out of the Body* is said to have popularized the term "out-of-body experience," or OBE.

Monroe's original objective had been to develop a process by which people could learn effortlessly—while they were asleep. He developed sound patterns that would help people reach a state that he called "Stage Two Sleep" and hold them in that state. Monroe experimented on himself and exposed himself to many varieties of sound. One night in 1956, quite unexpectedly, he found himself floating over his body. He panicked and thought the must be dying. He consulted medical doctors and psychiatrists about this, and eventually understood he wasn't dying—that this experience was fairly common. As a result, he conducted more experiments to learn how to replicate what he had done, and to control it.

By the time Monroe came to Skip's attention, he had established The Monroe Institute about 40 minutes by car from Charlottesville, Virginia, where the public could come to share in these sound-created experiences. Skip decided to investigate, and traveled from Fort Meade to Virginia to meet Monroe.

Skip, of course, was running a secret program for the U.S. Army and could not disclose the real reason for his visit. But he did explain to Monroe that he was interested in the work being done, had read his book, and had had out-of-body experiences as a child.

Monroe invited Skip to come into his laboratory. He took him to a room that had been set up and equipped for his experiments. He had Skip lie down. Skip became nervous. He was, after all, an intelligence officer on a surreptitious mission.

"What are these sounds I've heard about—these hemi-sync® sounds?" Skip asked.

"Oh, nothing to worry about," Monroe said. "I'll just play some music at first to calm you down."

As soon as Skip was lying down on the bed with the headphones on, the door shut and the lights went out. He wondered what he'd gotten himself into.

Music came through the speakers. It turned into the sound of surf against the shore. This reminded Skip of happy childhood days spent playing at the beach.

Then droning sounds came on in the background and quite unexpectedly the bed began to rise off the floor as though it were being lifted by hydraulics the way a car in a service station is lifted for an oil change.

Skip thought, "Wow, this is a very special bed. They must have one of those lifts underneath it to push it up in the air."

As he was thinking about what must have been done to build it—the building had to have been constructed around it—he began to feel himself moving in a different direction. He seemed to be headed laterally, rather than up. That's when he realized it must not be a lift he was on. Yet the feeling was very strong, quite visceral, as though he were on an airplane circling into a landing approach. He saw or imagined that he was moving through a rock or crystal tunnel of some kind. Then he heard a voice.

"Whoa, there. What's happening, kid?" It was Robert Monroe.

"Well, I seem to be going somewhere," Skip said.

"Well, now, where're you going, kid?"

"I don't know," Skip answered.

Skip traveled along the tunnel, or corridor, and eventually came out of it in vast, open, white space. He said it was a little like being in a white cloud except there was no mist or fog. Everything was white, boundless, and there were no walls.

Perhaps the strangest part was that Skip watched himself arrive.

He thought, Gosh, I've come all this way only to find I'm already here.

Skip said in our interview, "It sounds trite to say wherever you go, there you are, but that's exactly what happened to me."

He remained in the white space for a while. Then he heard Robert Monroe's voice again:

"What's happening?"

Skip was embarrassed because he'd forgotten he was in Monroe's laboratory lying on a bed.

He said, "Oh, nothing much."

"Okay . . . well, it's time for lunch."

This didn't make sense, but that didn't matter because Monroe changed the sounds coming through the headphones, and Skip felt the bed being lowered down to its original position. In a short time, the door was open and the lights were on.

Monroe was standing in the doorway.

Skip leaned over and looked under the bed.

"Oh, did you lose your wallet down there?" Monroe asked.

Skip was looking for the hydraulic lift, but there was none.

As a result of this experience, he learned there was definitely something to the sound technology Robert Monroe had developed, and the Army entered into a classified contract with Robert Monroe to do some training.

One man Monroe trained was perhaps the most outstanding remote viewer in the Army. His name is Joe McMoneagle.

Joe had been in intelligence before joining Skip's unit. His personal story is fascinating and was related to me by a guest on my show who'd gotten to know Joe over the years through an association with The Monroe Institute.

In the early 1970s, Joe was the target of a successful assassination attempt while in the Army stationed in Germany, working as an operative in intelligence. Poison was the method. He was meeting with an intelligence contact at a restaurant, having dinner, when he felt nauseous. He excused himself and went outside to get some air. He walked around for a moment, and then saw a crowd gathered just outside the door. He went to see what the commotion was about, looked through the crowd, and could make out a body lying on the street.

People were saying, "He's dead, he's dead!"

Joe came closer and was shocked to see the body was his own.

Testing later showed he'd been subjected to a binary poison, one that becomes toxic when combined with another substance. This had allowed his assassin to slip him the poison and make his getaway before Joe sat down to dinner and consumed whatever had triggered the toxicity that killed him.

McMoneagle's consciousness, after viewing his body lying on the street, went toward the light and through the tunnel described by many near-death survivors. As is now considered typical in these cases, he arrived at a place where he was met by spiritual beings. There, he underwent some instruction and a life review.

We would know nothing of this if Joe's body had not been resuscitated. His recovery and recuperation took quite some time.

What happened that evening changed Joe in several ways. He'd had psychic experiences before his NDE, but had kept them to himself. He no longer did. He also began to have spontaneous out-of-body experiences he was unable to control.

Joe's case came to the attention of two physicists at the

Stanford Research Institute, Russell Targ and Harold Puthoff. They'd already been working on a government contract to study the ramifications of the quantum mechanics theory of non-locality of consciousness. These were the same experiments described in the classified document found by Skip Atwater, and the same two men who'd authored the book he'd read.

Joe became the first remote viewer directly on the government payroll. In the course of his career in the Army as a remote viewer, Joe worked on more than 200 missions, many of which were reported at the highest levels of the U.S. military and government. Some of the information was considered so crucial, vital and unavailable from any other source, that he was awarded the Legion of Merit for his work, the second highest award the Army can give to someone in the military during peacetime.

One such mission was to determine the time and the location Skylab would fall to earth. Depending on how old you are, you may recall Skylab—literally a scientific laboratory in orbit around the earth, put there for astronauts to conduct experiments in space. Launched in 1973, it weighed about 100 tons.

By 1979 its orbit was decaying and Skylab was expected to come down. The question was, "Where?"

A hundred ton metal object falling on a heavily populated area such as New York, Tokyo or London, for example, would cause a tremendous death and destruction. Super computers were enlisted to answer the question, but too many variables existed for the technology of the day. The results were unreliable.

Joe McMoneagle, Ingo Swann and a third individual, a woman whose name I have been unable to uncover, were contracted individually to come up with an answer. None of the three knew the others were involved. All picked the same day, July 11, 1979, and almost the same time. Each was within five minutes of the other two—a location in western Australia, which was a remote, uninhabited area. These predictions were made nine and a half months before Skylab actually came down.

Skylab came down there, all right, almost precisely as predicted, demonstrating awareness is not located just inside our skulls. It also appears not to be limited in time—which, of course, cannot be possible according to the foundational principle of Scientific Materialism.

That thought is not confined to the brain, is nonlocal and has also been demonstrated by a gentleman I interviewed on my podcast named Stephan A. Schwartz. He is the author of several books including *Opening to the Infinite, The Alexandria Project,* and *The Vision: A Novel of Time and Consciousness.* He demonstrated this with an experiment that indicates that mind is everywhere at once and that thoughts are not electromagnetic waves. In other words, thoughts do not travel between minds like cell phone or radio signals between a sender and a receiver. The results of Schwartz's experiment suggest they apparently exist in a universal, perhaps foundational or underlying mind that we all share at a deep level.

Schwartz had researchers in a submarine lowered in water to a depth below which it has been demonstrated that electromagnetic waves—regardless of their frequency or strength—simply cannot penetrate. Remote viewers in the submarine were able to get the same results with respect to targets located on the surface as were remote viewers who were located on the surface.

Telepathy [ESP] experiments were also conducted. The results achieved by researchers in the submarine with those on the surface were comparable to the results achieved by a control group of researchers, all of whom were on the surface. This demonstrated that telepathy has nothing to do with electromagnetic waves. In other words, ESP does not work by messages traveling though space from one mind to another. This suggests that what mystics have been saying for millennia is correct: All Is One. Being located in a submarine deep below the surface of the ocean doesn't change this. Details of this experiment can be found in Schwartz's book, *OPENING TO THE INFINITE: The Art and Science of Nonlocal Awareness* (Nemoseen Media, 2007).

I must say the implications of all this are difficult to wrap one's thoughts around. Mind apparently transcends time and does not occupy space. It appears to be everywhere at once in a universal and eternal now. It also seems to me that consciousness is life and that life is consciousness. You can see this by closely observing nature. Consider a sunflower. It has no brain.

According to currently accepted science, it can have no awareness. Yet it turns its face to the sun, and it follows the sun across the sky from sunrise to dusk. Plants of all kinds search for and grow toward the sun. Like it or not this requires some form of awareness.

Scientifically constructed, double blind experiments by researchers, including Nobel laureate and theoretical biophysicist of the University of Marburg in Germany, Fritz-Albert Popp [1938-2018], have demonstrated that plants are aware, and this isn't news. About 40 years ago a fellow named Cleve Backster [1924-2013] demonstrated plants are aware by using polygraph machines. In Backster's most famous experiment, he hooked up plants in his office suite to polygraph machines, and then set up a device to randomly dump a cup of living brine shrimp into a pot of boiling water. The needles on the polygraph machines would go wild each time the shrimp hit the water and went to their deaths. I've seen videos of this experiment on national television. The only logical explanation is that the plants were picking up the shrimp's distress and demise.

But what led Cleve Backster to construct and carry out this experiment may be even more of an eye-opener. Lynne McTaggart, author of *The Field: The Quest for the Secret Force of the Universe,* told the following story on my show early in 2008.

Backster was an expert on polygraph machines and their operation—in other words, lie detectors. One evening when Backster was a young man, he was sitting in his office with nothing much to do. His eyes fell on an office plant and he had an idea. He decided to hook up one of his machines to the plant and see if he could get it to react. He connected the machine and poured a glass of water into the soil around the plant. Nothing happened. The polygraph registered boredom.

Backster started thinking about what he might do to get a reaction out of the plant, and he had an idea.

"I think I'll burn one of its leaves."

At that moment, the polygraph machine went wild. The plant had reacted to his thought! The more Backster thought about burning the plant, the more the needle on the polygraph machine went ballistic.

Cleve Backster conducted many experiments along these lines which are described in his book, *Primary Perception: Bio Communication with Plants, Living Foods, and Human Cells* (White Rose Millennium Press, 2003).

People who have what's called green thumbs may think it is because they send kind thoughts to their plants. It may be true that kind thoughts help make happy plants, but as we now know, thoughts are not sent and received. Thoughts just are. They are located in the mind that we and every other living thing share.

In the next chapter, we will examine what the role is of our brains.

Chapter Five: The Role of the Brain

Let me extend my apologies to you if you have read my book, *Afterlife, Powerful Evidence You Will Never Die.* In this chapter, I'm going to summarize a lecture I also summarized in that book. It was recorded on video given in India in 2011 by Bruce Greyson, M.D., who at the time was The Chester Carlson Professor of Psychiatry and Director of the Division of Perceptual Studies at the University of Virginia whose job it was to study consciousness. Dr. Greyson, as you recall, was the young psychiatrist who had the spot on his tie.

The bottom line takeaway of Dr. Greyson's lecture is that brains do not actually create consciousness, despite what many scientists think. Rather, the brain is a receiver of consciousness, and its role is to integrate your consciousness with your body. In other words, what some now refer to as the "body-brain complex" is a mechanism that allows you, a spiritual being, to operate in this (physical) reality.

Dr. Greyson did say in his lecture, however, that the mistaken belief that the brain creates consciousness is understandable since evidence does exist that the brain produces consciousness. Consider what happens when a person drinks too much or gets knocked on the head. Also, it's possible to measure electrical activity in the brain during certain kinds of mental tasks and to identify correlations between different areas of the brain and the different activities. We can stimulate different parts of the brain and record what experiences result, and we can remove parts of the brain and observe the results on behavior. This suggests that the brain is involved with thinking, perception, and memory, but according to Dr. Greyson, it does not necessarily suggest the brain causes those thoughts, perceptions, and memories. What the measurements actually show are correlations, rather than causation. The truth is that thoughts, perceptions, and memories, actually occur somewhere else and then are received and processed by the brain in a way similar to how a television, cell phone, or radio receiver works.

Western science, Dr. Greyson pointed out, is largely reductionist. It breaks everything down to its component parts, which are much easier to study than the whole, but the component parts do not always act like the whole. The brain is composed of millions of nerve cells or neurons, but a single neuron cannot formulate a thought, cannot feel angry or cold. It appears that brains can think and feel, but brain cells cannot. No one knows how many neurons are needed in order for them to collectively formulate a thought, nor do we know how a collection of neurons can think when a single neuron cannot.

Scientists get around this by saying consciousness is an emergent property of brains, a property that emerges when a large enough mass of brain cells gets together. According to Dr. Greyson, however, saying something is an emergent property is a way of saying it is a mystery that cannot be explained. It is a fact that there is no known mechanism in the brain or anywhere else that can produce non-physical things like thoughts, memories, or perceptions. The materialistic understanding of the world fails to deal with how electrical impulses, or a chemical trigger in the brain, can produce a thought or a feeling, or for that matter, anything the mind does. Despite this, according to Dr. Greyson, most scientists continue to maintain what he labeled, "The nineteenth century, materialist view that the brain in some miraculous way we do not understand produces consciousness." These scientists, he said, "Discount or ignore that consciousness in extreme circumstances can function very well without a brain."

Dr. Greyson noted that the idea that the mind and the brain are separate is what most people believed until a couple of hundred years ago, but in the nineteenth century western world, beginning with the Darwinians, science began exploring the idea that the physical brain might be the source of thoughts and consciousness. Ironically, as one group of scientists attempted to explain consciousness in terms of Newtonian physics, scientists in a different discipline, physics, were forced to move away from Newtonian physics and develop quantum mechanics in order to explain phenomena in which consciousness—what a researcher knows or doesn't know—completely changes the results of certain experiments. It is as though the right hand did not know what the left hand was up to. Incredibly, this remains how things are today.

Dr. Greyson listed a number of examples in his lecture of evidence researchers with the Division of Perceptual Studies—established in 1967 at the University of Virginia—have collected that demonstrate that consciousness can exist without a brain being involved. It is a testament to the stubbornness of materialist scientists that even though Dr. Greyson and his colleagues have been collecting this data for fifty years, and many papers and books have been written and published revealing a great deal of it, most western scientists are unaware of this evidence. As a result, you will soon have a leg up on many western scientists.

The evidence falls into four categories:

1. Recovery of lost consciousness in the moments or days prior to death among people who have been unconscious for prolonged periods of time.
2. Complex consciousness ability in some people who have minimal brain tissue.
3. Complex consciousness in near-death experiences when the brain is not functioning or is functioning at a greatly diminished level.
4. Memories, particularly among young children, accurately recalling details of a past life.

Deathbed recovery of lost consciousness

The unexpected return of mental clarity shortly before death by patients suffering from neurological or psychiatric disorders has been reported in western medical literature for more than 250 years. There are published cases in the medical literature of patients suffering from brain abscesses, tumors, strokes, meningitis, Alzheimer's disease, schizophrenia, and mood disorders, all of whom long before had lost the ability to think or communicate. In many of these cases, evidence from brain scans or autopsies showed their brains had deteriorated to an irreversible degree, and yet in all of them, mental clarity returned in the last minutes, hours, and sometimes days before the patients' deaths. The Division of Perceptual Studies has identified 83 cases in western medical literature and has collected additional unpublished contemporary accounts wherein patients recovered complete consciousness just before death. It appears as though the damaged brain released its grip on a patient's mind and clarity returned as a result.

In 1844, a German psychiatrist named Julius reported that this occurred in 13 percent of patients who had died in his institution. In a recent investigation of end of life experiences in the United Kingdom, 70 percent of caregivers in nursing homes reported that they had observed patients suffering from dementia and confusion becoming completely lucid in their last hours before death. In a case Dr. Greyson himself investigated, a 42-year-old man developed a malignant brain tumor that rapidly grew in size. He quickly became bedridden, blind in one eye, unable to communicate, incoherent and bizarre in this behavior. He appeared unable to make any sense of his surroundings, and when members of his family touched him, he would slap as though being annoyed by an insect. He eventually stopped sleeping and would talk deliriously throughout the night making no sense. After several weeks of this, he suddenly appeared calm and began speaking coherently. He then slept peacefully. The following morning, he remained completely clear and talked with his wife, discussing his imminent death for the first time. He then stopped speaking and died.

There is no known physiological mechanism to explain this phenomenon. It is rare, but the fact that it happens has no explanation in terms of how the brain functions. It suggests the link between consciousness and the brain is more complex that most scientists think. It is as though the damaged brain prevents the person from communicating, but when the brain finally begins to die, consciousness is released from the degenerating brain.

Complex consciousness among people who have minimal brain tissue

Another phenomenon is the presence of normal or even high intelligence in people who have very little brain tissue. There are rare but surprising cases of people who seem to function normally, with normal intelligence, and normal social function, despite having virtually no brain at all. In one case, published in 2007, a high school honor student who had been accepted for enrollment by Smith College underwent surgery after she was injured and knocked unconscious in an automobile accident. An x-ray of her head just before surgery revealed that she had no cerebral cortex at all. She had just a brainstem inside her skull. When the surgeon opened her skull to operate that is exactly what he found—a brainstem and that's all.

Neurologists tell us the brainstem relays motor and sensory signals to the cerebellum and the spinal cord and integrates heart function, breathing, wakefulness, and animal functions. They also tell us the brainstem does not have the connections to perform higher cognitive functions such as thinking, perceiving, making decisions, and so forth. According to scientific knowledge as it now stands, this college-bound honor student should not have been able to formulate a thought of any kind, let alone function at a high intellectual level.

Hers is not an isolated situation. Dr. Greyson pointed to dozens of cases of patients with hydrocephalus, wherein as much as 95 percent of a brain is incapacitated due to an excess of cerebrospinal fluid, and yet many with that level of affliction have normal and even above average intelligence.

Near Death Experiences

The near death experiences [NDEs] Dr. Greyson covered in the lecture were accounts given by people who had been clinically dead for a short time and then resuscitated or revived spontaneously. He said they typically have memories of vivid sensory imagery, and an extremely clear memory of what they experienced. They often describe what they experienced as seeming "more real" than their everyday life. All of this occurs under conditions of drastically altered brain function under which the materialist model would say is absolutely impossible. Such memories are reported by between ten and twenty percent of those who are revived from clinical death. Dr. Greyson has personally investigated almost one thousand cases.

The average age at the time of the near death in these cases was 31 years, but there was a very wide range. A young girl reported an experience she'd had at eight months old while undergoing kidney surgery. The oldest to experience near death Dr. Greyson has studied was 81 at the time of his heart attack. About one third of the NDEs occurred during surgical operations, a quarter during serious illness, and another quarter as a result of life-threatening accidents. The common features of NDEs can be categorized as changes in thinking, changes in emotional state, as well as paranormal and otherworldly features.

Changes in thinking include a sense of time being altered. Often people report that time stopped or ceased to exist. The change in thinking phenomenon also included a sudden revelation or change in understanding in which everything in the universe suddenly became crystal clear. There was a sense of the person's thoughts going much faster and being much clearer than usual. Finally, there was a life review—a panoramic memory in which the person's life seemed to flash before him or her.

Typical emotions reported included an overwhelming sense of peace and wellbeing, a sense of cosmic unity and of being one with everything, a feeling of complete joy, and a sense of being loved unconditionally.

The paranormal features included a sense of leaving the physical body, sometimes called an out of body experience [OBE], a sense of physical senses such as seeing and hearing becoming more vivid than ever before. Sometimes people report seeing colors and hearing sounds that do not exist in this life, and a sense of extrasensory perception, i.e., of knowing things beyond the normal ability of the senses, such as things that are happening at a remote location. Finally, some report having visions of the future and that they entered another, unearthly world or realm of existence.

Many report they came to a border they could not cross, a point of no return that if they had crossed they would not be able to return to life. Many also say they encountered a mystical or divine being, and some report seeing spirits and loved ones who died previously and seem to be welcoming them into another realm, or in some cases sending them back to life.

As a psychiatrist, the profound after effects of NDEs are of particular interest to Dr. Greyson. Near death survivors reliably report a consistent pattern of changes in attitudes, beliefs, and values, which do not seem to fade over time. They report overwhelmingly they are more spiritual because of their experience, that they have more compassion, a greater desire to help others, a greater appreciation for life as well as a stronger sense of meaning and purpose in life. A large majority reports they have a stronger belief that we survive death of the body and no longer fear death. About half report they have lost interest in material possessions, and many report they no longer have an interest in obtaining personal prestige, status, or in competition.

Dr. Greyson said that three features of NDEs suggest consciousness is not produced by the brain: 1) Enhanced mental function while the brain is incapacitated; 2) Accurate perceptions from outside the body, such as the ability to accurately tell doctors and nurses what they saw and heard going on in the operating room; and 3) encounters with deceased persons who convey accurate information no one else could have known, including in some instances encounters with deceased persons the NDE survivor could not have known were dead at the time.

In one case, a nine-year-old boy with meningitis had an NDE in which he saw several deceased relatives, including his sister who told him he had to return to his body. As soon as he returned from death, he told his parents—who had been at his bedside for 36 hours during his ordeal. His father became very upset because his daughter was at college in a different state and was perfectly healthy as far as the father knew. The boy insisted that his sister had sent him back and had told him she had to remain.

The father left the hospital, promising his wife he would call their daughter as soon as he got home. When he tried to call her, he learned that the college officials had been trying to contact him and his wife all night to tell them the tragic news. Their daughter had been killed in an automobile accident around midnight.

By the way, if you would like to see a video of Dr. Greyson's lecture just summarized, go to YouTube and search "Dr Bruce Greyson consciousness independent of the brain." A video of the lecture should come up at the top of the list.

Children Who Recall a Past Life

Dr. Greyson also recounted information about the Division of Perceptual Studies' research into children's memories of past lives. Researchers at the University of Virginia have been conducting these investigations for more than fifty years and as a result have in excess of 2500 cases in their files. I was quite familiar with this even before I saw Dr. Greyson's lecture because of research I had done for my book, *REINCARNATION: Good News for Open Minded Christians and Other Truth Seekers.* I have in fact twice interviewed one of the Perceptual Division's key researchers who has written two books on the Division's reincarnation research findings, Jim B. Tucker, M.D., a child psychiatrist.

Anyone with an open mind who looks into what has been found will find it difficult to refute that reincarnation can and does happen. To give you a taste, I will relate a fascinating case history I also reported on in the book just mentioned. This true story began on the First of May 2000.

Imagine you and your wife [or husband] are sound asleep. Your two-year-old son James is in his crib, asleep in the next room. Suddenly you are jarred awake.

You hear your son scream, "Plane on fire! Airplane crash!"

You rush into his room, and there he is on the bed, writhing the grip of horror, kicking and clawing at the covers as if he is trying to kick his way out of a coffin.

Over and over again, your child screams, "Plane on fire! Little man can't get out!"

What happened that night was not a single occurrence. Traumatic nightly scenes like it became the norm. The nightmares became even more terrifying, and James started screaming the name of the "little man" who couldn't get out of the plane. It was "James," his own name. Other words he spoke out loud included: "Jack Larsen," "Natoma" and "Corsair."

James' father, Bruce Leininger, could not think of what to do. Eventually, in attempt to find an answer to his son's troubled nights, he embarked on a research project, armed only with the names and words his son had been shouting while in a disturbed sleep.

A devout Christian, the answer Bruce found was not the one he wanted. He came to believe his son James was the reincarnation of a World War Two fighter pilot whose plane had been hit and downed by antiaircraft fire—a pilot named James Huston who had died in 1945 after his plane suffered a direct hit and crashed.

James' mother, however, was the first to suspect the truth. At the time, James was having five nightmares a week, and his mother, Andrea, was worried. At a toy shop, Andrea and James were looking at model planes.

"Look," Andrea said. "There's a bomb on the bottom of that one."

"That's not a bomb, Mommy," James said. "That's a drop tank."

The child was two years old. How could he possibly have known about the gas tank used by aircraft in World War Two to extend their range?

As the nightmares continued, Andrea asked, "Who is the 'little man'?"

"Me," he answered.

Bruce asked, "What happened to your plane?"

"It crashed on fire."

"Why did your plane crash?"

"It got shot," James said.

"Who shot your plane?"

"The Japanese!" he said.

James said he knew it was the Japanese because of "the big red sun." He was, of course, describing the Japanese symbol of the rising sun painted on their warplanes.

Andrea began to suggest reincarnation. Wouldn't that explain it? But Bruce reacted angrily. He thought there must be a rational explanation, and reincarnation was definitely not in his mind a rational explanation.

Bruce questioned his son further. "Do you remember what kind of plane the little man flew?"

"A Corsair," two-year-old James replied without hesitation. It was a word he had shouted in his dreams.

Bruce knew a Corsair was a World War Two fighter plane.

"Where did your airplane take off?" Bruce asked.

"A boat."

"What was the name of the boat?"

James replied with certainty, "The Natoma."

Bruce did some research. He was amazed to find the Natoma Bay was a World War Two aircraft carrier. Bruce rushed to his office, where he had a dictionary of American naval fighting ships. Natoma Bay had supported the U.S. Marines' invasion of Iwo Jima in 1945.

Andrea, meanwhile, had become convinced James was reincarnated. She contacted Carol Bowman, the author of a book on reincarnation and children who remember past lives. Bowman confirmed Andrea's views, saying that the common threads were there with James, including his age when the nightmares began and his remembered death.

Bruce kept investigating. He decided to see if he could find someone named Jack Larsen, a name James had shouted repeatedly during his nightmares. Bruce was successful in finding someone who fit the time period and place. It turned out Larsen's friend James Huston had died when his plane was shot in the engine and caught fire, just as had been described by two-year-old James Leininger.

Bruce also found Huston's name on the list of 18 men killed in action on the Natoma. The discovery finally made him realize his son might actually be the reincarnation of James Huston. But he kept investigating, anyway, and everything he found served to confirm that conclusion.

One day, little James unnerved his father when he said, "I knew you would be a good daddy, that's why I picked you."

"Where did you find us?" asked an incredulous Bruce.

"In Hawaii, at the pink hotel on the beach," James said, and went on to describe his parents' fifth wedding anniversary, which had taken place five weeks before Andrea had gotten pregnant. James said that was when he "chose" the couple to bring him back into the world.

Something new emerged almost every day. On a map, James pointed out the exact location where James Huston's plane went down. Asked why he called his action figures "Billy," "Leon" and "Walter," he replied, "Because that's who met me when I got to heaven."

Eventually, the family received a phone call from a veteran who had seen Huston's plane get hit. The man had kept his knowledge to himself for more than 50 years. He described seeing the aftermath of Huston's crash on the sea below.

"He took a direct hit on the nose. All I could see were pieces falling into the bay. We pulled out of the dive and headed for open sea. I saw the place where the fighter had hit. The rings were still expanding near a huge rock at the harbor entrance."

And so it was as James had said. His plane was hit in the engine and the front exploded in a ball of flames, but that was not the end of James. He returned to this reality fifty-three years later, in 1998, with his memory intact. Perhaps he had some things here on earth he wanted to do, like flying airplanes.

How about you? Whether you come back to this world, stay in the next or move on to another, like it or not it appears you are likely to continue to exist. If you didn't believe that before, how will that change your outlook on life?

Chapter Six: Sixty Years of Research

I spoke with someone on my podcast in March 2009 who believes in reincarnation based on almost sixty years of meticulous study—although not all of it his own. I mentioned him in the previous chapter. His name is Jim B. Tucker, and he is a Phi Beta Kappa graduate of the University of North Carolina, a medical doctor, a board certified child psychiatrist and the Bonner-Lowry Professor of Psychiatry and Neurobehavioral Sciences at the University of Virginia School of Medicine.

As you now know, the Division of Perceptual Studies at the University of Virginia Medical School has been researching the subject of children's memories of past lives since the 1960s. Much of this work was done by, or under direction of, the late Ian Stevenson, M.D. (1918-2007), who wrote a shelf full of books on the subject, having compiled more than 2500 such cases. At the time I spoke with Dr. Tucker, about 1600 of these had been entered into a computer database along with the information collected on each. This was sorted into about 200 different variables, allowing researchers to comb through and cross tabulate the data to spot trends as well as to categorize and compare the similarities and differences based on various factors and characteristics.

Dr. Stevenson was a methodical and meticulous researcher who graduated first in his medical school class at Canada's McGill University. He never actually claimed reincarnation as fact, but rather, said his cases were "suggestive" of reincarnation. His often-cited first book on the subject was published in 1966 and entitled, *Twenty Cases Suggestive of Reincarnation.*

The cases he studied come from all over the world. When Dr. Stevenson began this research, they were easiest to find where people have a belief in reincarnation such as India and Thailand. This may be because parents were not as likely to think a child was imagining a past life, and because they are not likely to be embarrassed to talk about it. Nowadays, however, people in the United States are not as reticent as they once were. Dr. Tucker says that since the University of Virginia set up a web site on this subject, he and his colleagues hear from parents "all the time" about their children's memories of past lives.

Nevertheless, in the United States reincarnation is thought by many to go against Christian doctrine—reincarnation was eliminated from Christian canon at the Council of Constantinople in 553 by what was reportedly a close vote of the bishops present. Even so, recent surveys show that more than twenty percent of Christians believe in reincarnation, and the percentage is higher among younger adults.

In one case Dr. Tucker studied, an 18-month-old child told his father, who was changing his diaper, that he had changed his father's diaper when he was his father's age. The child's mother was the daughter of a Southern Baptist preacher, and so, as you might imagine, she found what her son said to be highly unusual. I asked Dr. Tucker to describe the case when he came on my show, and he obliged.

The child's grandfather had died eighteen months before the child's birth. His first mention of having been his own grandfather was during that change of diapers, but as time went by he made more comments about how he used to be big, and what he did when he was. His mother in particular became interested and began to ask the boy, whose name was Sam, questions. Sam came up with some very specific statements. For instance, she asked him if he had had any brothers or sisters. He said he had had a sister who was killed. In fact the grandfather's sister had been murdered sixty years before. The parents felt certain the child could not have known this since they had only recently learned about it themselves.

The child also talked about how, at the end of his previous life, his wife would make milkshakes for him every day, and that she made them in a food processor rather than in a blender. This turned out to be true.

When Sam was four years old, his grandmother—his wife in his previous life—died. Sam's dad traveled to where she lived and took care of the estate. When he returned, he brought some family photos with him.

One night Sam's mother had the pictures spread out on the coffee table. Sam walked over and pointed to pictures of his grandfather and said, "Hey, that's me."

To test him she pulled out a class photo from the time the grandfather was in elementary school. Sam ran his finger across the photo, which had sixteen boys in it, and stopped on the one who had indeed been his grandfather.

"That's me," he said.

Dr. Tucker told me he thought the grandfather may have come back as the son of his own son because of the relationship—or lack thereof—the two had had in his previous life. The grandfather had not had an open relationship with Sam's dad. He had been a very private person. Sam's dad felt that if his father had really returned as his son, his father may have decided to come back to try to develop a closer bond than had existed in their previous relationship. Dr. Tucker said this might be true. When he visited the family he could see that Sam and his dad were very close.

Another interesting case Dr. Tucker related on my show had to do with an Indian girl named Kum Kum, who said she had been murdered in her previous life—poisoned—by her daughter-in-law. Kum Kum said she was from a city of about 200,000 located about 25 miles away. One of the things that makes this a good case is that her aunt wrote down a number of statements—eighteen in all—she made before an effort was undertaken to see if they checked out.

All of them did.

The statements included the name of a son, the name of a grandson, the fact that the son had worked with a hammer. And a number of other specifics—for example, that she had a sword hanging near the cot where she slept, and a pet snake she fed milk to.

Research led to the woman Kum Kum claimed to have been, who had died five years before she was born. A big family flap had taken place over a will and who would inherit the worldly possessions of the deceased woman's son. Kum Kum had probably been right. Circumstantial evidence indicated the son's wife had poisoned her mother-in-law—the woman Kum Kum insisted she'd been.

These case histories are fascinating and convincing, and we could go on almost indefinitely considering each one, individually. After all, there are more than 2500 in UVA's files. Instead, let's step back and look at the overall findings of this exhaustive study.

Children who report past-life memories typically begin talking about a previous life when they are two to three years old. Emotional involvement with past-life family members would seem to indicate reincarnation rather than superpsi or the psychic reservoir at work in that the children tend to show strong emotional involvement with their memories and often tearfully ask to be taken to the previous family. Once there, not only is a deceased individual usually identified whose life matched the details given, during the visits, children often recognize family members or friends from that individual's life. Tearful reunions are common.

Many children studied also had birthmarks that matched wounds on the body of the deceased individual. One example is that of a boy in Thailand who said he'd been a schoolteacher in his previous life and was shot and killed when riding his bicycle to school one day. He gave specific details including his name in that life and where he had lived. He continued to make this claim until his grandmother took him to the previous address, and the child was able to identify the various members of his previous family by name. Even more startling, however, he was born with two birth marks: a small round birthmark on the back of his head and a larger, more irregularly shaped one near the front. The woman he claimed had been his wife in that life recalled investigators saying her husband had been shot from behind. The investigators said they knew this because he had a typical, small, round entrance wound in the back of his head and a larger, irregular exit wound in front.

In another case, a boy remembered a life in a village not far away in which he had lost the fingers of his right hand in a fodder-chopping machine. The child was born with an intact left hand but the fingers of his right hand were missing.

The average length of time between the death and rebirth of the children in the birthmark cases is only fifteen to sixteen months. It has been theorized that this sort of thing may happen when the reincarnating entity takes a shortcut between lives, skipping a process by which the life just lived would have been fully integrated into what may be a higher self—in religious terminology, "the soul"—of an individual that remains always in the nonphysical realm. According to Dr. Tucker's book, *Life Before Life* (St. Martin's Griffin, 2005), about 22 percent of the cases in the University's database include birth defects due to wounds suffered in violent deaths in the previous life. Most of the cases come from the Hindu and Buddhist countries of South Asia, the Shiite peoples of Lebanon and Turkey, the tribes of

West Africa, and the tribes of northwestern North America.

In 1997 Stevenson published details of 225 cases in a massive work *Reincarnation and Biology: A Contribution to the Etiology of Birthmarks and Birth Defects.* The same year he presented a summary of 112 cases in a much shorter book, *Where Reincarnation and Biology Intersect.*

In many cases postmortem reports, hospital records, or other documents were located and consulted that confirmed the location of the wounds on the deceased person in question matched the birthmarks. These often correspond to bullet wounds or stab wounds, and as in the case described above. Sometimes two marks correspond to the points where a bullet entered and then exited the body.

Birthmarks were also related to a variety of other wounds or marks, not necessarily connected with the previous personality's death, including surgical incisions and blood left on the body when it was cremated. A woman run over by a train that sliced her right leg in two was reborn with her right leg absent from just below the knee. A man born with a severely malformed ear had been resting in a field at twilight, mistaken for a rabbit, and shot in the ear.

Further evidence for reincarnation comes from what might be called behavioral memories. For example, cases exist where children of lower caste Indian families believe they had been upper class Brahmins, and in their view still were. These children would refuse to eat their family's food, which they considered polluted. Conversely, a child remembering the life of a streetsweeper—a very low caste—showed an alarming lack of concern about cleanliness. Some children demonstrate skills they have not learned in their present life, but which the previous personality was known to have had. A number of Burmese children who recalled being Japanese soldiers killed there during World War Two preferred Japanese food such as raw or semi-raw fish over the spicy Burmese fare served by their families.

Many children express memories of their previous life in the games they play. A girl who remembered a previous life as a schoolteacher would assemble her playmates as pupils and instruct them with an imaginary blackboard. A child who remembered the life of a garage mechanic would spend hours under a family sofa "repairing" the car he pretended it to be. One child who remembered a life in which he had committed suicide by hanging himself had the habit of walking around with a piece of rope tied round his neck.

Phobias occur in about a third of the cases and are nearly always related to the mode of death in the previous life. For example, death by drowning may lead to fear of being immersed in water; death from snakebite may lead to a phobia of snakes; a child who remembers a life that ended when he was shot may display a phobia of guns and loud noises. A person who died in a traffic accident may have a phobia of cars, buses, or trucks.

Sexual orientation may also be affected by a previous life. In one of his books, Ian Stevenson wrote, "Such children almost invariably show traits of the sex of the claimed in the previous life. They cross-dress, play the games of the opposite sex, and may otherwise show attitudes characteristic of that sex. As with the phobias, the attachment to the sex and habits of the previous life usually becomes attenuated as the child grows older; but a few of these children remain intransigently fixed to the sex of the previous life, and one has become homosexual."

Certain preferences and cravings can also carry over. They frequently take the form of a desire or demand for particular foods not eaten in the child's present family, or for clothes different from those ordinarily worn by the family members. Other examples include cravings for addictive substances, such as tobacco, alcohol, and other drugs that the previous personality was known to have used.

Dr. Tucker pointed out that the cases he and others have studied might not be typical because most children do not remember past lives. As mentioned, the average time between lives in these cases is only fifteen months or so—although there are outliers that range up to fifty years. In 70 percent of these cases, the previous personality died by unnatural means. Many died young. This may speed up the reincarnation process. The consciousness may come back quickly due to unfinished business, or because he or she feels shortchanged. The quick return may also be the reason past life memories are intact, as well as sexual preferences, cravings and so forth. My guess is that a much longer duration between lives is the norm.

Chapter Seven: Who You Are

We have seen that life could not have come about if an incredibly powerful intelligence hadn't created the DNA molecule and arranged the code in it in a way that would cause it to produce specific types of proteins just at the right times. We have also seen that there is only one intelligence and one life. To paraphrase Gary Zukav's famous conclusion quoted earlier, quantum mechanics tells us that everything in the entire universe including you and me—everything that seems to exist independently—is in reality all one single, all-encompassing whole. Nothing is separate. As mystics have been saying for millennia, *all is one.* This implies that there is one single mind as well. Consciousness, the medium of mind, permeates reality, as the previously-discussed experiment conducted by Stephan A. Schwartz using a submarine demonstrated. Even plants are conscious. The minds of researchers cause the results of quantum mechanics experiments to change. Remote viewers can use their minds to see what's happening at great distances, even into the future and the past. Mediums can communicate with loved ones who have passed from the physical plane.

This begs the question, "Who and what are you?"

The answer is, "You are consciousness itself. Your consciousness and my consciousness—everyone's consciousness is the ground of being consciousness we all share. We are all one being, each of us with our own memories and personalities that cause us to think we are separate and apart from one another and the whole, but we are not—not at the core. Our seemingly separate minds blend into the One Mind. The twentieth and twenty-first century findings related in this book demonstrate this. We are eternal, nonphysical beings having temporary physical experiences.

I could go on, but the truth is clear, and here it is:

We are each the Creator experiencing the reality we have created for ourselves.

The great twentieth century prophet, Edgar Cayce (1877-1945), often said, "Spirit is the life, mind is the builder, and the physical is the result." These few words describe the formula behind the existence of the physical world and all its trappings, you and me included. Spirit is the life. It is consciousness, the force that animates living creatures. It is imbued with a raw organizing intelligence that formed the stars and the planets out of nebulae. It organized atoms into RNA, and later DNA, molecules. Mind is the builder. The mind creates thoughts. Thoughts are things that exist in spirit, and what exists in spirit will in time exist on the physical plane.

It seems logical to me that we humans and everything else in the universe evolved out of the organizing intelligence that is spirit. In the beginning, spirit created an almost infinite number of variations of living things. Here's one way I imagine evolution might have progressed. Those that were most suited to the environment survived. These living things reproduced by the millions, each offspring slightly different from its siblings. Again, those best suited to the environment survived and reproduced. And so on and so on. As evolution progressed, living organisms themselves developed intelligence, what in more highly evolved creatures such as humans are known as minds, conscious, unconscious, and subconscious minds. This intelligence impressed itself upon the organizing intelligence of spirit, and the organizing intelligence of spirit went to work to create ever more sophisticated and evolved adaptations. The result of this process can be seen in ever-increasing levels of intelligence displayed by ever more evolved life forms.

As intelligence evolves, it becomes more self-aware. Flowers and earthworms possess only subjective or subconscious minds, their own small portions of underlying organizing intelligence. Their "minds" are subjective because they cannot think about themselves. They can only react in a programmed way to the input or stimuli they receive. A dog and to a much greater extent, a human, have both a subjective mind and an objective mind. Their subjective minds keep them breathing and their bodies functioning while their objective minds think about and analyze situations. Unlike the subjective mind, an objective mind can worry and be afraid. This is both a blessing and a curse. It is a blessing that we can plan ahead in order to avoid trouble and thereby eliminate the uncomfortable sensation of worry. It is a curse because fear is a kind of belief—a belief charged with emotion. Since it does not analyze or judge, the subjective mind works hard to bring about what the objective mind believes. A fear is almost certain, therefore, to manifest if it is allowed to continue unchecked—whether or not that particular fear was originally grounded in reality.

As stated above, that there is only one mind because at some point, as we have seen, all minds blend. This is why remote viewing is possible. Psychics are able to push their minds past barriers that separate them from the whole. Like the vast majority of water on earth that is connected but divided into oceans, seas, and rivers, we can think of the one mind as being connected but divided into various levels: the universal subjective mind, the collective subconscious mind of humanity, individual subconscious minds or souls, and last but not least the part of each person's mind of which he or she is aware, the conscious mind. Our personal conscious minds in turn are divided into a conscious portion and an unconscious portion that contains the memories of this life and unconscious and habitual programming.

At the core, however, we are all aspects of the Infinite Mind, consciousness itself. We are all linked together, all one at the core, and that means we each are the Creator, the Source, experiencing our creation, as was stated above.

It may be shocking to realize that is actually who you are, but consider this. Would you agree it's impossible for you to be something that you can observe? For example, you are not the tree you can see across the street. You are not the house or apartment in which you live. You are not a penny on a sidewalk.

What you can observe includes more than objects. For example, although they may give you a sense of personal identity, you are not your job, you are not the country in which you were born, and you are not your religion. You are also not the color of your skin, and you are not the school or university you went to.

You are not your hands or your feet, and you are not your body.

"Wait. I'm not my body?"

That statement may raise doubt in you, but you are not something you can observe, and you can observe your body. In fact, the two words, "your body," suggest your body is not you, but rather, something that belongs to you. You can control the actions of your body. For example, you might decide to force it to dig a ditch, and if you do, after a few hours, you might say, "My body aches." And so it's not you that aches—it's your body—your back and your arms.

How about your mind? Do you think you are your mind?

You are not your mind, your mind is something that was built up over time, and, as you will see, realizing you are not your mind will empower you. Consider this. You can observe your thoughts as they come and they go. You may even observe them to a fault when they keep you awake at night. But you, the real you, do not have to be at the mercy of your thoughts, and therefore, your mind. Like Scarlett O'Hara, you can decide to think about tomorrow whatever problem has arisen in your mind today.

It's a fact. Anything you can—sometimes figuratively speaking—stand back and observe cannot possibly be you. Moreover, whether you realized it or not before now—whether you have ever exercised this prerogative or not—you can decide which thoughts to pay attention to and which ones to discard. You can decide what to think about, or not to think about. In other words, you can control the actions of your mind, just as you can control the actions of your body, and this means your mind cannot possibly be you.

You may be surprised to learn that you are the Creator, and you may initially experience an impulse to reject the fact, so consider this: There was a time when people thought the world was flat and that the earth was at the center of the universe—that the sun and the stars revolved around the earth. Now, just about everyone knows the earth is round, that the sun is at the center of the solar system, and that our solar system is one of trillions upon trillions.

Once you get in touch with and live your life from the viewpoint of your true Self, the eternal you at the core that is the Creator, once you truly accept and embrace the secret of life, you will live in peace and be free from suffering and desire. This will not require learning reams of information about spiritual matters and metaphysics. It will simply require setting aside the ego and realizing that you and God, or Source—what Jesus called the Father—are one and the same like peas in a pod. Jesus knew this and tried to explain it to anyone who would listen. We will review what he said about that, but first let me tell you the true story of someone I know who learned the secret of life and how it happened. I'll call him George.

Leading up to that day, George had been extremely unlucky in love. What he wanted more than anything was to be in love and to share a truly loving relationship, but at the age of 26, he had already suffered one failed marriage and two unfortunate, long-term relationships. The third breakup sent George into a deep and dark depression. He became suicidal, and except for work, spent two months alone in his apartment, much of it in a fetal position. He didn't see anybody. He didn't talk to anybody. The only thing he did to try to bring himself out of his depression was to listen to Eckhart Tolle podcasts and videos.

If you are not aware of Eckhart Tolle, he is a spiritual teacher and best-selling author, a German-born resident of Canada best known as the author of *The Power of Now* and also, *A New Earth: Awakening to Your Life's Purpose.* Tolle's essential message is to stay in the "Now" as much as possible. Rather than dwell on past problems or worry about what you might face in the future, the way to achieve peace is to step back from those thoughts and observe your own mind objectively, distinguish between the voice of your ego and your actual situation, and live as much as possible in the present moment—what Tolle referred to as the "Now." Tolle doesn't call it this, but from where I sit, he talks and writes about becoming enlightened.

During lunch and other breaks at work, George would find a quiet, secluded place on a bench outside his office building in the campus style business park where he worked. He would eat a sandwich, play Eckhart Tolle videos, and stare up at the sky. After a month or so of watching white, puffy clouds drift by, and listening to Tolle talk, he began to break free from his depression.

One day he was listening to a video and Tolle was saying things a voice in someone's mind might say that would bring them down, such as, "I'm no good. People laugh at me behind my back." The sarcastic way Tolle was saying these things caused his audience to laugh.

"Life is my enemy. It's treating me so unfairly. If only life would just be nicer to me." Everyone present with Tolle laughed again. Eckhart Tolle laughed, too, and this time George chuckled.

Then Tolle said, "If only I could have that one thing—then I would be truly happy!"

Everyone laughed, and it suddenly struck George that Tolle was talking about him. The inner voice Tolle was mimicking was the voice of his ego—the voice he had been hearing in his head saying if he could only find true love, he would be happy. Unless he did, he would simply have to remain miserable and depressed!

This struck George as so obvious it was hilarious, and he began laughing a sidesplitting, keeling-over laugh. For the first time, he saw through the petty game the ego plays and realized the thought voices weren't actually coming from him. The voice in his head was just some sort of automatic, conditioned-into-him response, a learned-mechanism from his past—his upbringing, his parents, his previous relationships. It was an old tape that played over and over, and it had been torturing him for months—perhaps even years—and the amazing thing was, he didn't have to listen to it. He could ignore it, or better yet, he could simply shoo it away.

This insight came to him in an instant. He realized he had fallen victim to a trap, and with that realization, he was free of it. Free! He laughed and the laughter brought an incredible sense of freedom because he was laughing at his ego, and his ego was an automaton that wasn't him. It was a construction built up over years—fueled by memories he did not have to identify with, and didn't have to let bother him if he didn't want them to.

After a few moments, his laughing turned into crying—not sad tears, but tears of joy, tears of relief. The small self mind noises of the ego self had been muted. He had simply stepped out of the poor-sad-guy-who-just-can't-find-love-boohoo-poor-little-me role he had unwittingly taken on, a role he despised, and he could now move on. He'd been caught in a trap—a mind mechanism trap that now had collapsed, leaving him to revel in beautiful, peaceful silence.

What George finally got in touch with was his true Self, his "I Am" that is pure and simple consciousness—the Silent Observer that was always there at the back of his mind, and is at the back of your mind—at the back of everyone's mind. It is the Creator, the core of each of us that is never stained by experience; never damaged. It does not age. It is not born. It does not die. It always is—the ground of being of All-That-Is.

George realized that to find it, you have to do what Jesus said to do in Luke 9:23-24 (NIV):

> *Whoever wants to be my disciple must deny themselves and take up their cross daily and follow me. For whoever wants to save their life will lose it, but whoever loses their life for me will save it.*

George realized that Jesus meant by telling disciples they must "deny themselves," He was saying they needed to deny their small selves, their ego selves, and identify with the "I AM" part of them—the ground of being in each of us from which Jesus lived and operated. In other words, it struck George that to truly follow Jesus, one had to jettison the ego and live from the perspective of the One Life that so filled Jesus, i.e., that one must empty oneself of the small self in order to fill oneself with the Big Self—the Divine Self at our core some refer to as "the Silent Observer."

George also realized that our personal identity, our ego, is like a filter we see reality through. It causes us to live under the illusion that we are defined by our circumstances and environment, which is why everyone sees reality differently. Most of us view the world through a filter—our unique lens. The only way to see true reality is to see it from the Big Self, and so the more identified and attached we are to our little identities, the less clearly we see and the more clouded everything becomes. Unfortunately, our judgments, our awareness, our clarity can become extremely clouded, and when that happens, we suffer, and often we cause the world around us to suffer with us.

Here is the intended message of what is written above: If you want freedom, if you want liberation from psychological suffering, if you want surcease of sorrow and desire, if you truly want the truth, then you must shoo away the small, ego you, which is a false you, and make it disappear. When you do, the Real You—the "I AM" that is your window to the One Mind—will appear.

This is often accomplished through meditation. When meditating, ego thoughts are pushed away, ignored, or simply observed as irrelevant or perhaps even amusing BS by the Real You, the Silent Observer.

If you do not engage in meditation now, I suggest you give it a try. Go on YouTube and watch a few videos that give you pointers. Spend ten minutes to half an hour in meditation every morning or evening—perhaps even both. If you do that for a while, it may become a habit you look forward to. Be aware, however, that at first your ego mind will object and attempt to torpedo your efforts because it fears annihilation. Remember, the ego is in the business of survival, and so it will keep telling you that you are wasting your time. Don't let it have the upper hand. Keep pushing ego thoughts away or ignoring them. Eventually, if you want liberation and enlightenment enough, the Real You will overcome and the ego's screaming out in the throes of death will fade away.

Chapter Eight: The Real You

Christians believe that Jesus was God incarnate, and that is true. However, it is also true that each and every one of us—you included—is God incarnate. Consider this. In Chapter Ten of the Gospel of John, Jesus explained that it wasn't he but the "Father," i.e., what Christians typically assume was God working through him that caused the miracles with which he was credited. As part of his explanation he said, "I and the Father are one." (See John 10:30 NIV.) This got him into trouble with Jews who became angry and were about to stone him.

Jesus replied to the angry mob by saying, "I have shown you many good works from the Father. For which of these do you stone me?" (John 10:32 NIV)

The Jews answered, "We are not stoning you for any good work, but for blasphemy, because you, who are a man, declare yourself to be God." (John 10:33 NIV)

Jesus then quoted Psalm 82:6: "Is it not written in your Law: 'I have said you are gods'?" (John 10:34 NIV)

By quoting this Scripture Jesus clearly was indicating that the Jews who wanted to stone him were "gods," as was he and every other human being—and that includes you regardless of the color of your skin or whether you are a Christian, an atheist, or a follower of Islam. The reason people think it is impossible that God is within us and that we, like Jesus, are God, is that for millennia our culture has bought into the idea that God can be compared to a man with a long white beard lounging on a cloud up in the sky—that he is a separate entity. But he is not. He is everywhere—the ground of being. All truly is one, seamless whole. It is impossible to go anywhere where God is not.

By the way, I invite Christians who may scoff at this, or who think I am the one guilty of blasphemy, to consider these words also spoken by Jesus: "Whoever believes in me will do the works I have been doing, and they will do even greater things than these . . . " (See John 14:12 NIV) To believe in Jesus means, among other things, to believe what he said and taught is true, and that requires believing that we must have the ability, as he said in the Scripture just quoted, to perform miracles. Once we fully become fully evolved beings, as Jesus was, we will be able to do so.

Jesus also famously said, "Anyone who has seen me has seen the Father" (See John 14:9). Christians take that statement to mean Jesus was saying he was God incarnate. And he also said, "When you have done it unto the least of these you have done it unto me." (See Matthew 25:40.) Christians have a difficult time figuring out what he meant by that, but it becomes obvious when those two statements are put together that Jesus understood that we all are one, and that the "I AM" at the back of our minds is the window on the One Life that is God.

Jesus was all, just as I hope you will come to recognize that you are all.

How can you wrap your mind around this and accomplish it? How do you come to recognize and feel at a deep level that there is no separation from you, others, and God? I suggest you spend time every day when you're out in the world seeing other people as simply yourself in another body. That may seem difficult and perhaps silly at first, but after a while, it will do wonders for opening your heart to the world and to universal love. Seeing others as an extension of yourself will bring peace of mind and help mitigate your suffering in difficult situations. Moreover, you cannot truly serve others with deep compassion unless you see them as part of yourself.

Let me interject here that once you realize you and others are one, you do not have to become a pushover or a doormat. If people want to steal from you, or loot your business, for example, it is correct to stop them. Oneness means that others are no less the Creator than you, but it also means they are no more the Creator than you. Treating others as you want to be treated is the right way for everyone to behave, and that means that if someone treats you in a way you don't want to be treated, you are obligated to speak your truth and stand up for yourself.

What I am hoping to communicate is what was discussed in the previous chapter and what George realized: That All-Is-One, and your consciousness, my consciousness, and indeed everyone's consciousness is the single, unified, underlying "I AM" consciousness that Jesus called his "Father." It is the infinite consciousness that underlies, supports, informs—and indeed creates physical reality. You don't have to be religious to understand that—you just have to open your eyes and your mind. It is what Jesus understood, and that understanding and with powerful belief is what gave him the ability to work miracles. When that has been taught in school for a couple of generations, and everyone realizes it, racism, poverty, and suffering will become greatly diminished.

That we are each the Creator experiencing our creation is not a new idea. Alan Watts [1915-1973], a twentieth century philosopher and interpreter of Zen Buddhism, answered children's questions concerning why they were here, where the universe came from, where people go when they die and so forth with a parable about God playing hide and seek. Watts told them God enjoys the game, but has no one outside himself to play with since he is All-That-Is. God overcomes the problem of not having any playmates by pretending he is not himself. Instead he pretends that he is me and you and all the other people and the animals and rocks and stars and planets and plants and in doing so has wonderful and wondrous adventures. These adventures are like dreams because when he awakes, they disappear. Here is some of what Watts wrote:

> *Now when God plays hide and pretends that he is you and I, he does it so well that it takes him a long time to remember where and how he hid himself. But that's the whole fun of it—just what he wanted to do. He doesn't want to find himself too quickly, for that would spoil the game. That is why it is so difficult for you and me to find out that we are God in disguise, pretending not to be himself. But when the game has gone on long enough,*

all of us will wake up, stop pretending, and remember that we are all one single Self—the God who is all that there is and who lives forever and ever.

It will no doubt be shocking to some to think of themselves as God, but Watts was talking about the core essence that is beyond the ego and deeper within than the personal unconscious, the collective unconscious, the archetypes and so on. As Joseph Campbell [1904-1987] said in the PBS TV series, *The Power of Myth,* "You see, there are two ways of thinking 'I am God.' If you think, 'I, here in my physical presence and in my temporal character, am God,' then you are mad and have short-circuited the experience. You are God, not in your ego, but in your deepest being, where you are at one with the non dual transcendent."

As indicated above, that we are all One Life that arises from the "non dual transcendent" is not something I came up with. Mystics and enlightened men and women have known this for thousands of years. In the text that follows, I am going to touch on a theory I have written about in other books. In the Appendix of this book is a section from one of those books that goes into much more detail. I put it there for you to read if you are interested.

Two mysteries have captivated the human imagination for thousands of years. The first is why the universe exists at all. Why is there something rather than nothing? The second is that conscious minds exist to perceive it. An ancient idea is that the mystery of consciousness and the mystery of existence are intimately connected, and perhaps surprisingly, a growing number of philosophers and scientists now take this possibility seriously. Apparently, science is finally waking up to the truth.

Beginning in the first half of the twentieth century, cosmologists began learning a great deal about the early universe by analyzing cosmic background radiation and other phenomena. Using powerful telescopes they were able to see that there are many galaxies, and due to their shift toward the red end of the spectrum of light, that those farthest away are moving away from us faster than those in closer proximity. As a result, cosmologists are able to peer deeply into the past and infer the state of the universe in what is thought to be its first fractions of a second. But where did it all come from? What existed before the beginning?

Physicists have proposed that the spark of existence had its origin in a quantum fluctuation, triggering an explosive chain reaction, leading to the still evolving universe we inhabit today. This narrative, however, presupposes the laws of quantum mechanics. As British Biochemist Rupert Sheldrake said in a now banned TED Talk, "[Scientists today say] give us one free miracle and we'll explain the rest.' And the one free miracle is the appearance of all the matter and energy of the universe, and all the laws that govern it, from nothing in a single instant." Suffice it to say that rather than explaining existence, current scientific theories of the origins of the universe have simply pushed things back to a point that raises the question, "What existed before the beginning?" Could it all have come from nothing? Although that is apparently what some scientists believe, it doesn't make sense. As the song in *The Sound of Music* goes, "Nothing comes from nothing, nothing ever could."

Instead of beginning with nothing, it seems logical that the challenge of explaining existence should focus instead on defining a self-existing ground of being for which no explanation is required. Some physicists have proposed that the true ground floor of reality is the seething quantum realm of particles, forming in and out of existence. While this level of reality surely exists, there is no clear reason why the primordial situation should be constrained by quantum physics. A deeper level of explanation seems to be required, and one possibility is that consciousness is the ground of being. How seething quantum particles came to be the ground of reality calls out for an explanation, but in theory, consciousness can explain itself, and as Stephan A. Schwartz's experiment using a submarine apparently demonstrated, consciousness—the medium of mind—is everywhere at once, which is what one would expect if it is the ground of being of physical reality. Moreover, a unique feature of consciousness is that it does not appear grounded in anything beyond itself. The conscious self is self-producing in so far that it exists only in and to itself. As René Descartes [1596-1650] famously said, "I think therefore I am." In other words, nothing is required beyond consciousness for existence to be a demonstrated fact.

Your consciousness seems to belong to the person you consider yourself to be because you have memories stored in your unconscious mind. You also have a name and perhaps a job and a history that was created while inhabiting your current physical body. You may think of yourself as American, Canadian, British, or Australian. Perhaps you grew up poor, or maybe your father was the CEO of a Fortune 500 company. The skin that covers the body you now inhabit might be black, white, brown, or some shade in between. Perhaps you subscribe to Christianity, Judaism, or Islam. You might have been a good student, or not so good, a star quarterback on the high school team, or a 98 pound weakling. The combination of all that gives you a sense of identity—it's who you think you are—your ego. But none of that is who you actually are, and your ego is not you.

As George realized, the ego is a construction, and it is not in the business of eliminating your suffering—quite the contrary. The ego is concerned only with its own survival. It wants to be in charge, and as such, causes you to react the way you do to outside stimuli—it is what makes you feel bad, sad, angry, or fearful. Give it some thought and you will realize your ego is not your friend.

You might think of the ego as a computer program like the one in the movie, *The Matrix,* that prevents you from seeing reality as it truly is. It won't allow you to see your true potential, which is virtually unlimited. The ego causes your psychological suffering. But now you know the truth: you don't have to obey the ego's demands to react to situations as you do today. Besides taking advantage of the moment between stimulus and response to stop and think before you react, you can wake up and realize who you really are—you are the Source in disguise experiencing your creation. You can become whatever you can truly come to believe yourself to be because of what some now call the Law of Attraction, Christians call the Law of Reaping and Sowing, and in the East is known as the Law of Karma. There's a wonderful little book written by a man named James Allen [1864-1912] that drives home this point. It's called, *As a Man Thinketh.* I highly recommend it.

You may recall a British Biochemist named Rupert Sheldrake mentioned earlier who wrote a book called *A New Science of Life*. That book put forth a theory that what he called "morphogenetic fields" work together with an animal or a human's genes to form and shape the embryos that develop in mothers' wombs. Suffice it to say that you began as a spark of the Source and evolved a morphogenetic field—what is also known as an etheric body—over a period of billions of years to become a self-aware entity that has a subconscious mind or soul that contains all the memories of your past incarnations. You will continue to have the memories of this life when your consciousness leaves your current body—if not indefinitely, at least until those memories merge into your subconscious mind or Soul.

When you rejoin the Creator at the end of your evolutionary journey and all levels of your consciousness merge into the

Universal Consciousness, that universal consciousness will be you, and you will still be aware. I say this because, as you now know, consciousness is the Silent Observer at the back of your mind. The "I AM" or Creator that is the real you. Knowing that should erase any fears that may be troubling you.

That you are eternal, and the best is yet to come, ought to bring you a sense of pure joy. Think about that. Savor it.

In the next chapter we will accompany an explorer of the vast reality we inhabit but do not see while encapsulated in a physical human body.

Chapter Nine: Robert Monroe's Journeys

You may recall that Skip Atwater, who founded the and led the U.S. Army remote-viewing spy unit called Stargate visited The Monroe Institute [TMI] located not far from Charlottesville, Virginia, and that TMI personnel trained Stargate personnel in remote viewing techniques. TMI remains active today and is dedicated to helping others safely do what Robert Monroe and the Stargate psychics were able to do through the use of sound technology.

According to its website, TMI's mission is "Helping people create more meaningful and joyful lives through the guided exploration of expanded consciousness." Reportedly, thousands have followed Monroe's path, apparently verifying in their own minds that consciousness is the larger reality. I have interviewed several individuals who maintain that they have visited The Monroe Institute and done so themselves.

What Robert Monroe says he did and wrote three books about appears to lend credence to the assertion that consciousness is fundamental and the ground of being of all that is. Monroe was not a scientist, nor was he a mystic or a philosopher. He was a successful network radio executive—logical, practical, deeply rooted in the physical world. Monroe's reports are experiential narratives, not laboratory findings. They are presented here as models that attempt to shed light on questions about consciousness and the larger reality raised earlier. They are not presented as scientific proof.

As touched upon previously, one evening he unexpectedly experienced, and later continued to experience, something I believe most people will agree a machine will never be able to do. He left his body. It happened while he was in bed experimenting with sleep-learning and sound frequencies that were designed to enhance memory. Inexplicably, he began feeling vibrations and a sense of detachment. Then he left his body and looked down at it.

Initially, he feared that was dying or losing his mind, but after it happened several times, he began experimenting with the phenomenon. Through practice and persistence, Monroe said he learned how to leave his body whenever he wanted to, and what had begun as a frightening anomaly became a discipline—a way to separate from his physical body while maintaining consciousness.

He began doing so on a regular basis and kept meticulous notes, approaching each journey like a scientist studying an undiscovered frontier. As time went by, he began to map what he encountered. He discovered that nonphysical reality was not chaotic but structured—layered like levels of consciousness, which he later called "Focus Levels."

At first, he stayed close to Earth. He floated through his house, visited distant friends, even attempted to influence objects. These experiences were vivid and verifiable enough to convince him that he was not dreaming.

Later, he ventured farther, beyond the realm of the living where he encountered vast and varied planes of existence. He met those recently dead, still clinging to earthly habits and confusion. He found regions of serene light where guides and helpers worked to ease souls' transitions. And farther still, he entered abstract realms—zones of pure thought and energy where individuality blurred into unity.

Monroe's explorations transformed his understanding of life and death. He came to a conclusion that seems similar to Max Planck's, that *consciousness* is the fundamental reality. He also concluded that we are not bodies that possess souls, but souls that temporarily wear bodies, that death is not the end, that death is merely a shift in focus, a transition from one layer of experience to another.

He met beings who guided him, some human in form, others that were radiant beyond description. They showed him that every soul undergoes cycles of learning and return—incarnation not as punishment, but as opportunity. Each lifetime was a classroom where love, compassion, courage, and creativity were lessons in the curriculum of growth.

In later journeys, Monroe wrote that he learned to navigate the nonphysical realms with precision. He developed techniques—eventually forming the basis for his *Hemi-Sync* audio technology—to help others reach altered states safely. This is what visitors to The Monroe Institute near Charlottesville, Virginia, experience when they visit there. What had begun as a personal odyssey became a mission to teach humanity that consciousness is far more vast than we imagine.

Monroe's travels and research led him to believe that all beings are part of a single vast field of intelligence—the Source, the Creator, or as he sometimes called it, the Gathering. He came to believe that the universe is evolving toward reunion with the Source and that each soul contributes to this through its experiences and emotions.

Monroe's views of the unfolding of the universe grew with time and his many out of body journeys. This can be seen clearly in the three books he wrote, brief summaries of which are below:

Journeys Out of the Body — The Discovery

In *Journeys Out of the Body* (1971), Monroe told the story of his first steps beyond the known world. The early experiences were filled with astonishment and fear—sensations of vibration, a rushing sound, the sudden awareness of floating free from the body.

He explored tentatively at first: his own room, the houses of friends, even places miles away, all while his physical body lay sleeping. Sometimes he verified what he saw—a clock's position, an object out of place—and came to believe he was operating in a real dimension, not in an imaginary one.

In those early days, he encountered both beauty and confusion. There were shadowy zones filled with drifting, lost minds—people who had died but did not know it—and luminous regions filled with serenity and guidance. Monroe struggled to understand what he was seeing, calling it "Locale I" (close to Earth) and "Locale II" (a nonphysical universe of vast scale).

Far Journeys — The Mapping

By the time he wrote *Far Journeys* (1985), Monroe had become a seasoned traveler. The shock of discovery had faded and the scientific mind within him had taken over. He began to classify and chart the realms he encountered, organizing them into "Focus Levels"—gradations of consciousness from the physical world outward to the highest planes of awareness.

Now his journeys took him far beyond Earth's influence. He met beings of intelligence beyond human measure—"Helpers" and "Gatherers," entities working in harmony with the evolution of souls. He saw the Earth as part of a vast system—a living training ground where consciousness grew through experience.

It was during this phase that Monroe was shown the "Parable of Loosh," the energy of life generated through emotion and experience. The story seemed to indicate that existence was an experiment—a cosmic garden producing energy through love, loss, and growth, which is akin to the Christian Gnostic idea that humans have been trapped in physical reality by a lesser god, the Demiurge, and that entities called Archons feed off the emotions of trapped human souls. Yet Monroe's tone was not dark. It was analytical, even reverent. He saw humanity's struggles as part of a grand design—the Creator's way of evolving through its own creation.

He also encountered what he called "the Gatherings"—immense collectives of nonphysical beings observing Earth, waiting for a great turning point. Something was coming, Monroe was told, a shift in human consciousness that would radiate far beyond this world.

In *Far Journeys*, Monroe became a cartographer of the invisible, laying down maps for those who would follow. But he was still the observer—the reporter. He had not yet become the participant in the great drama he described.

Ultimate Journey — The Integration

By the time Monroe wrote *Ultimate Journey* (1994), he was no longer merely traveling through other realms. He was remembering them. The explorer had discovered that the lands he mapped were not foreign at all, but parts of himself.

He came to believe that each of us has what he called an "I-There"—a greater Self composed of all our lives, experiences, and incarnations. He viewed each lifetime as a probe sent into different times and conditions to learn and return with wisdom. The I-There gathered all this experience into wholeness, growing ever closer to the Source from which he wrote that all consciousness arises.

In this book, Monroe no longer spoke of Loosh as energy to be harvested but as love unfolding. The universe was not a farm but a school, not a mechanism but a living being seeking reunion with itself.

He journeyed beyond all levels—even beyond the collective of I-Theres—into what he called the Aperture, and there he sensed that the Source was an infinite, conscious presence that was both the beginning and the destination of all journeys.

The explorer had reached the farthest shore—and found home. Monroe returned from his final journeys with a message distilled from decades of exploration:

> You are more than your physical body.
> You are not alone.
> There is purpose.
> There is continuation.
> There is growth.
> There is love.

Chapter Ten: The Spiritual Renaissance

Across the world, interest in consciousness, spirituality, and the nature of life beyond death of the body has been increasing. This hasn't been happening so much within traditional religious frameworks. Rather it is taking place through psychology, philosophy, personal inquiry and those searching to discover and understand the true nature of reality, which is what I have been doing for half my life

There seem to be a couple of reasons this is happening. Artificial Intelligence and what may come along with it is partly responsible, but the big one is that Scientific Materialism, aka Physicalism, leaves a number of questions unanswered.

I do not view this movement as a retreat from science. Quite the contrary. I see it as an expansion of science. As external, surface explanations reach their limits, people naturally begin exploring the internal dimension of life, and it seems to me that the rise of AI is accelerating the process.

If Monroe's writings, near-death research and other findings reported upon are pointing toward something real—even if consciousness can only exist independent of the brain in part—then it may be foundational—not a product, not a side effect, but a fundamental aspect of reality. In spite of all the evidence presented in this book, however, this remains an open question, and so I suggest that you decide for yourself what you think is true.

In this chapter and the next we will review the work of what might be described as unconventional researchers—back in the twentieth century they would likely have been dismissed by physicalists as kooks. Today, I believe that what they had to say is worth considering based on what you have read in the previous chapters.

Let's start with Edgar Cayce, who lived from 1877 to 1945 and was known during his time as "The Sleeping Prophet." He is perhaps the most documented psychic of all time because the accuracy of his pronouncements tended to check out with uncanny accuracy. I interviewed several recognized authorities on Edgar Cayce and his readings in 2007, including his son, Edgar Evans Cayce [1918-2013] who related several fascinating stories about his father that he personally witnessed.

Edgar Cayce was a devout Presbyterian and Sunday school teacher who read the Bible once through for every year of his life. For more than 20 years he would twice per day—morning and afternoon—put himself into a self-induced trance and answer questions, the answers to which were transcribed by a stenographer. The original documents are housed in a building owned by the Association of Research and Enlightenment [A.R.E.] at the corner of 68th and Atlantic Avenue in Virginia Beach, Virginia, the nonprofit organization Edgar Cayce founded in the 1930s.

Most of his readings had to do with medical problems doctors had been unable to cure. But many, more than 2000 of the total 14,000-plus readings, had to do with the big questions, such as the meaning of and purpose of life. Whether one accepts Cayce's cosmology or not, it represents one of the most detailed modern attempts to articulate a teleological account of human existence. If you would like to know more about Cayce and what his readings revealed than will be disclosed here, you may want to read my book, *Edgar Cayce, The Meaning of Life & What to Do About It.*

According to Cayce's psychic readings, the story of human life does not begin on Earth, nor does it end with death. It begins in spirit—before time as we measure it existed. That's when souls, including yours and mine, were created by the Source—"God" if you prefer—as conscious, willing beings, aware of their divine origin and free to participate in creation itself. In this original state, souls existed in harmony with God, yet they were without the depth of self-knowledge that comes only through experience. They *knew* God, but they did not yet know themselves *as separate* from God. And it was precisely this possibility—the capacity for individual choice—that set our long journey in motion.

Cayce described a primordial moment, not as a fall imposed from above, but as a decision souls made for themselves. Endowed with free will, they chose to explore selfhood apart from constant awareness of the divine presence. This choice was not evil in intent. It was experimental—an extension of curiosity, creativity, and independence. Yet it carried with it consequences. As attention turned outward and inward simultaneously, souls gradually moved away from pure spiritual vibration and toward form, energy, and eventually matter.

Incarnation did not occur all at once. According to Cayce, souls first interacted with subtler levels of form before becoming fully incarnated in physical bodies. As identification with material experience increased, souls became increasingly bound to dense vibration. Earth, prepared for this purpose, became a school—a place where spirit could encounter limitation, resistance, and consequence, and through them, develop discernment.

The human body, in this view, is not the soul's identity but its instrument. It is a vehicle chosen, shaped by prior experience and present intention, suited to the lessons a soul seeks to learn. Circumstances of birth—family, culture, talents, challenges—are not random assignments but meaningful contexts, selected before incarnation to address unfinished growth and to provide opportunities for service.

Thus, the purpose of earthly life is neither punishment nor reward. It is for the implementation of a predetermined mission. Cayce returned to this theme repeatedly: ideals known in spirit must be *lived* in matter. Love must be practiced under pressure. Patience must be exercised amid frustration. Faith must be expressed where certainty is absent. Knowledge alone does not transform the soul. Choice does.

Within this framework, good and evil are not cosmic opposites locked in battle. Evil is not a force, but a condition—misalignment between the soul's choices and its divine origin.

Sin, Cayce said, is simply "missing the mark." Suffering arises not from divine wrath, but from the friction created when will moves out of harmony with universal law. And suffering, crucially, is corrective rather than punitive. It persists only until understanding is gained.

Death, then, is not a judgment or an ending. It is a shift of focus. When the physical body is laid aside, the soul returns to nonphysical realms that reflect its inner state. Awareness continues. Memory returns. As many near-death experiencers report was the case for them, the just-lived life is reviewed—not by an external authority, but by the soul itself, now able to see clearly the effects of its choices on others and on its own development.

Post-mortem realms are not fixed heavens or hells. They are states of consciousness, temporary conditions through which the soul rests, studies, assists others, and prepares for further experience. Growth does not cease at death; it continues.

Reincarnation, a staple of Cayce's cosmology, is the mechanism that makes divine justice both compassionate and complete. Souls return to Earth again and again—not endlessly, but as needed—until balance is restored and lessons are integrated. Memory of past lives is usually veiled, not as punishment, but to preserve freedom. Without forgetfulness, choice would become constrained by fear, regret, or attachment. Each life must be lived freshly, even as it builds upon all that came before.

Through many lifetimes, the soul gradually transforms self-centered will into alignment with divine will. The long arc of existence bends toward integration. No soul is abandoned. No error is permanent. Progress may be slow or resisted, but it is never denied.

The ultimate destination of the soul, in Cayce's readings, is conscious reunion with God—not absorption, not annihilation, but fulfillment. Individuality is not erased; it is refined. The soul becomes once again a conscious co-creator, now enriched by experience and wisdom freely chosen.

Cayce often referred to this state as *Christ consciousness*—not as an exclusive condition attained by one being alone, but as the natural culmination of every soul's journey. Jesus, in this view, was not an exception to the human story, but its clearest exemplar.

Seen as a whole, Cayce's cosmology presents human life as a purposeful passage through matter, guided by law, sustained by mercy, and directed toward eventual wholeness. Earth is neither a prison nor a proving ground imposed by God, but a classroom entered by choice. And the journey, however long it may take, ends not in judgment, but in remembrance.

To summarize what Cayce's readings say, human souls were created as spiritual beings who entered matter through free-will experimentation, incarnating on Earth to transform self-centered will into loving alignment with God, evolving through many lifetimes until consciously reunited with the Source—without loss of identity, without eternal punishment, and without exception.

In the next chapter we will consider what other ancient and modern prophets have to say about the soul's journey.

Chapter Eleven: More Views on the Human Soul & Evolution

If it's true that each of us really has already lived many times, then when our body dies and our consciousness returns to the nonphysical realm, who are we? Are we the person who just died? Are we a combination of our many previous lives? According to some who claim to know, we maintain our individual identity as part of an oversoul or higher self—and what Robert Monroe called the "I-There."

Monroe is not the only philosopher or theologian to suggest that each human being has a higher self or oversoul that embodies the wisdom and the memories acquired in many seemingly separate lives. It is a fact that a persistent theme can be seen across many spiritual and esoteric traditions. In this view, the part of us that we call "me," that which causes us to think "I am," is only a fragment or facet of something larger. You might say that our day-to-day consciousness is like a beam of light shining from a source we cannot see. That source—the "Higher Self," "Oversoul," "Atman," or "Inner Daemon"—holds the full memory, wisdom, and purpose of all our experiences across many lifetimes.

As mentioned in Chapter One, psychiatrist Carl Jung's *Wandlungen und Symbole der Libido*, known in English as *The Psychology of the Unconscious,* postulated a collective unconscious, sometimes known as collective subconscious.

According to Jung, this unconscious mind shared by all humanity is the product of the experiences of our ancestors, and it contains such concepts as the classic archetypes, science, religion, and morality.

As previously mentioned, Robert Monroe described the Oversoul—or what he called the "I-There" cluster—as a kind of multidimensional intelligence made up of many individual incarnations. Each lifetime might be thought of as a probe, a point of awareness sent out to gather experiences. In other words, these lives are not separate beings competing for attention, but complementary facets of one evolving intelligence.

Here are the key features of Monroe's view:

- Many lifetimes, one higher identity: Each incarnation is like a finger on the hand of a much larger Self.
- Shared learning: Experiences from each lifetime are absorbed by the Oversoul to increase its understanding.
- Nonlinear time: Incarnations may not occur in strict sequence; multiple "probes" can operate simultaneously.
- Gradual reintegration: When a lifetime ends, the personality does not vanish but merges into the fuller I-There, contributing its knowledge.

As you now know, Robert Monroe's beliefs were not formed through the study of philosophy or religious traditions. They are based on what he witnessed during his many journeys out of his body.

Verdantic Thought

In Vedantic thought, the individual soul (Atman) is a spark of the greater universal Self (Paramatman/Brahman), and it appears to forget its vastness when embodied, much as Monroe's probe-self sent forth forgets the I-There.

Here are the similarities to Monroe's beliefs:

One larger Self underlying many apparent selves
Reincarnation as a learning process
Ultimate reintegration with the greater Whole

And the differences:

Vedanta sees the larger Self as universal, not personal; Monroe depicts a unique oversoul with its own cluster of incarnations.
Vedanta frames reincarnation as a karmic cycle; Monroe sees it more as an educational exploration

Ralph Waldo Emerson, born 1803 and died 1882, though not speaking of reincarnation explicitly, described an Oversoul as a vast, shared spiritual reservoir connecting all human minds. In this vision, intuition is the whisper of this deeper, collective Self.

Overlap with Monroe:

A larger intelligence behind personality
Inner guidance as communication from that greater source

Difference:

Emerson's Oversoul is universal, not the personal reincarnation cluster Monroe described.

According to Monroe, in the beginning, if such a thing as a beginning can even be said to exist in a universe where time behaves more like a landscape than a river, there was a shimmer of consciousness. It was small only in appearance, the way a seed seems small although it contains an entire forest within itself. This was the proto-self, the heart of what would one day become an Oversoul.

It possessed an urge to experience, to know, to grow by becoming. And so this early Self moved outward from the larger field of consciousness into the realms of form and became the first "probe."

Imagine an explorer stepping into an unknown land. The moment the probe slipped into incarnation, it gained the sense of "I am." It did not remember the greater Self, because memory would bias its reactions to what it would encounter. It had to experience freely, innocently, without expectation.

It lived a life full of joys, sorrows, triumphs, and errors. At the end of that life, it returned like a traveler carrying a pack of treasures home to the hearth. Every memory, every emotion, every insight was absorbed and integrated into the larger Self. And the Oversoul grew. Not larger in size, but richer—more nuanced, more capable, more awake.

Monroe never preached a doctrine, but came to a quiet conclusion:

> *The purpose of the I-There is to grow into a fully conscious, self-determined unit of awareness that can participate creatively in the evolution of All-That-Is. Human lifetimes are like classrooms, and the Oversoul is the student. Graduation is the awakening of the whole cluster into a unified, powerful identity.*

From the perspective of the Oversoul, you—the personality reading these words—are not a small or temporary thing.

You are a beloved envoy, a sensory extension.
You are the frontier explorer of your greater Self.
Your joys deepen It.
Your pain enriches It.
Your questions sharpen It.
Your choices shape It.

If what is written above is true, when your life ends, you will go home—not to a deity separate from you, but to the greater

You that has been watching, waiting, and learning from your journey.

And one day, as Monroe suggested, you will awaken fully into that larger identity and say:

I remember. I am all of these. And now I will continue.

Ironically perhaps, I wrote a passage for a novel that without consciously realizing it reflects what is described in this chapter and the previous one. It must have resonated with readers because the novel won the *Writers Digest* Book Award for Fiction and First Prize for Fiction from *Independent Publisher.*

The book's title is *The Secret of Life: An Adventure Out of Body Into Mind*. The scene takes place when the protagonist of the story comes to a similar realization after an out of body experience during which she glimpsed the Eternal. The following internal dialog from that novel takes place after she has returned, and after she has described the experience to her boyfriend, Jeff, who has just told her she must have been dreaming:

> *I decided it didn't matter what Jeff or anyone else thought and turned my attention instead to the display of nature all around. A remnant of the glow of the light from the other side must still have been with me because I felt in awe as I took in the scene. We were passing giant bamboo, mountain palms, chestnut and mahogany trees,*

and were almost gulfed by foliage. It was hot and bugs swarmed and normally I'd have felt uncomfortable because of the temperature and the insects and the humidity, or perhaps I might even have been frightened by what I would have seen as an alien environment. Instead, I had the sensation of being part of it, of being one with it, the same feeling I'd had when I viewed the sunset from the motorcycle. The Life Force was expressing herself and I was seeing the outside of what was inside, the physical manifestation of the invisible: One Thing, completely and utterly connected. Then it came to me with the same unequivocal sense of knowing Jean-Luc had experienced during his revelation. I'd learned the secret of life. Of course, I thought, why hadn't I grasped it before? It is the urge to become I'd sensed in myself for as long as I could remember, which I now realized was the light's desire to express and experience itself. A vision flashed in my mind of a cave, a cavern like we have in the Blue Ridge Mountains of Virginia with millions of stalactites and stalagmites forming intricate and wondrous patterns glistening with tiny droplets of water. The whole was nature and each stalactite or stalagmite a separate soul, or species of plant or animal. Each had its own identity but was also part of the larger formation of rock. Every drop of water was a current life leaving in its path a tiny deposit that helped shape the species, or in the case of humans—the soul. At that moment I understood that the realm of my father's Higher Self was a metaphor his mind had created just as mine had created this cavern, and that his life, my life and your life are like those water droplets. They are expressions of the light and cause something larger to grow, a universe that is becoming. They are sent forth as knights were sent forth to the Crusades.

Chapter Twelve: Life as the Universe Experiencing Itself

For most of the modern scientific era, life has been understood as a curious accident of chemistry. According to the conventional account, the early Earth was once a lifeless world of rocks, oceans, and atmosphere. Over immense spans of time, complex molecules formed, organized themselves into primitive cells, and gradually evolved into the extraordinary diversity of organisms that inhabit the planet today. Through natural selection and genetic mutation, simple life forms slowly became more complex, eventually producing plants, animals, and finally human beings.

Within this framework, consciousness is generally regarded as a late and incidental development—an emergent property of biological brains that evolved because it helped organisms survive. Yet this explanation leaves a number of questions unresolved not the least of which is this:

If consciousness is merely a by-product of physical processes, why should the universe produce it at all?

Why should matter organized in a particular way suddenly give rise to subjective experience—the inner sense of being aware?

The question becomes even more intriguing when we consider the long trajectory of evolution. Over billions of years, life on Earth has moved steadily toward increasing complexity. The earliest organisms were simple cells barely capable of interacting with their environment. Later came multicellular organisms with specialized structures—organs for sensing, moving, and responding to the world around them. Eventually evolution produced nervous systems, brains, and the capacity for learning. In some animals, awareness of the surrounding environment became increasingly sophisticated.

Then, quite recently in geological terms, something remarkable appeared: self-awareness. Human beings are not only conscious; they know that they are conscious. We can reflect on our thoughts, contemplate the past and future, and ask questions about the nature of existence itself.

We can wonder why we exist. We can wonder what the universe is.

This development represents one of the most extraordinary transitions in the history of life. For the first time, the universe—through human consciousness—became capable of examining itself.

Some scientists and philosophers have suggested that this may not be a coincidence. If consciousness is fundamental rather than accidental, then biological life may represent the means through which consciousness explores the physical world. Under this interpretation, evolution is not merely a process by which organisms adapt to their environments. It may also be a process through which awareness gradually acquires more complex forms of expression.

Early life may have possessed only the faintest glimmer of awareness—simple responsiveness to environmental conditions. As nervous systems evolved, organisms gained richer sensory experiences and greater capacity for interaction, and with the emergence of complex brains, consciousness acquired the ability to form memories, anticipate events, and make choices. Finally, with the arrival of human beings, consciousness gained something entirely new: the ability to reflect upon itself.

As a result of this progression, it's possible to interpret evolution not only as the history of life but also as the history of awareness becoming increasingly capable of understanding its own existence. The French philosopher and scientist Pierre Teilhard de Chardin [1881-1955], for example, once described evolution as a process moving toward greater interiority—greater depth of awareness within living systems. Whether or not one accepts his broader philosophical conclusions, the pattern he identified is striking. As biological complexity increases, so too does the apparent richness of conscious experience. Simple organisms exhibit minimal responsiveness. Animals with nervous systems display perception, emotion, and learning. Humans demonstrate language, imagination, and abstract thought.

This correlation between biological complexity and conscious capacity raises an intriguing possibility. Perhaps the physical structures produced by evolution are not generating consciousness but allowing it to manifest in increasingly sophisticated ways. Just as a radio with more advanced circuitry can receive a wider range of signals, a more complex brain may allow a broader expression of awareness.

Under this view, biological organisms are not creators of consciousness but instruments through which consciousness interacts with the physical universe. Life becomes the interface between mind and matter.

This perspective would also shed new light on humanity's unique place in the evolutionary story. Among all known forms of life on Earth, human beings appear to possess the most developed capacity for self-reflection. We can examine our own thoughts, question our assumptions, and imagine realities beyond our immediate sensory experience. We can investigate the laws of physics. We can explore the origins of the cosmos. We can ask the deepest question of all: what is consciousness?

When we do so, something remarkable occurs. The universe begins to observe itself. The atoms that formed in ancient stars have assembled themselves into structures capable of awareness. Those structures—our brains and bodies—now allow consciousness to contemplate the very universe from which those atoms came. Seen in this light, the emergence of self-aware life may represent one of the most significant developments in cosmic history. Through living beings, the universe becomes capable of experience. Through intelligent beings, the universe becomes capable of understanding.

If consciousness truly is fundamental, then the appearance of life may not be a meaningless accident in an indifferent cosmos. It may be part of a deeper process through which reality gradually becomes aware of itself. From this perspective, the evolution of life takes on a new dimension. Biological complexity is not merely a sequence of physical adaptations. It may also represent the unfolding of consciousness into richer and more articulate forms. Human beings may be one stage in that unfolding.

We are not merely observers of the universe. We are participants in its ongoing exploration of itself. The question that began this inquiry—who we are and why we are here—may have an answer both simple and profound.

We are expressions of consciousness. We are the means through which the universe becomes aware of its own existence. Through the experiences of countless living beings—through curiosity, creativity, love, struggle, and discovery—the universe continues its extraordinary journey of self-understanding.

Chapter Thirteen: How You Create Your Personal Reality

Knowing you are at one with the All, and that you are the All is a magnificent feeling. Alan Watts, who apparently had achieved this state, wrote that at a gut-level, the realization of oneness brings moments of joy that are incredibly intense, that sorrows are looked upon philosophically, and that the sense of union with the universe empowers you. Once you come into harmony with all that is you will arrive in a position to live the totally fulfilling life you were born to live, and you will be positioned to achieve complete self-actualization. Here is a direct quote of some of what Alan Watts wrote about this:

> *In immediate contrast to the old feeling, there is indeed a certain passivity to the sensation, as if you were a leaf blown along by the wind, until you realize that you are both the leaf and the wind. The world outside your skin is just as much you as the world inside: they move together inseparably, and at first you feel a little out of control because the world outside is so much vaster than the world inside. Yet you soon discover that you are able to go ahead with ordinary activities—to work and make decisions as ever, though somehow this is less of a drag. Your body is no longer a corpse which the ego has to animate and lug around. There is a feeling of the ground*

holding you up, and of hills lifting you when you climb them. Air breathes itself in and out of your lungs, and instead of looking and listening, light and sound come to you on their own. Eyes see and ears hear as wind blows and water flows. All space becomes your mind. Time carries you along like a river, but never flows out of the present: the more it goes the more it stays, and you no longer have to fight or kill it.

When you know that All-Is-One and you are it, you will naturally want to "do unto others as you would have others do unto you." In an upcoming chapter, I will share some thoughts about how you might go about identifying your unique gifts and talents and how you might determine the most productive and satisfying way to put them to work in service to others. In the meantime, let's consider how your personal reality is created. If your circumstances and reality at present aren't what you would like them to be, let's also look at how you can create the circumstances and reality you would like to have.

It's a simple fact that beliefs—your beliefs and the beliefs of others—create your reality. This is so because belief—true, unadulterated belief—is powerful. The effectiveness of placebos, for example, has been demonstrated time and again in double blind, scientific tests. The placebo effect—the phenomenon of patients getting well or feeling better after taking dud pills—is seen throughout the field of medicine, and belief by a patient that he or she has taken real medicine is what causes it. One report says that after thousands of studies, hundreds of millions of prescriptions and tens of billions of dollars in sales, sugar pills are as effective at treating depression as antidepressants such as Prozac, Paxil and Zoloft. What's more, placebos cause profound changes in the same areas of the brain affected by these medicines, according to this research. For anyone who may have been in doubt, this proves beyond a doubt that thoughts and beliefs can and do produce physical changes in our bodies.

In addition, the same research reports that placebos often outperform the medicines they're up against. For example, in a trial conducted in April 2002 comparing the herbal remedy St. John's wort to Zoloft, St. John's wort cured 24 percent of the depressed people who received it. Zoloft cured 25 percent, but the placebo cured 32 percent.

Taking what one believes to be real medicine sets up the expectation of results, and what a person expects to happen usually does happen. It has been confirmed, for example, that in cultures where belief exists in voodoo or magic, people will actually die after being cursed by a shaman. Such a curse has no power on an outsider who doesn't believe. The expectation and belief causes the result.

Let me relate a real-life example of spontaneous healing that I believe came about because of her belief and that of others. It involved a woman I'd known for quite some time I will call Nancy, which is not her real name.

Nancy is a minister's wife. She's a devout Christian—as firm a believer in her religion as a bushman who'd drop dead from a witch doctor's curse is in his. Some years ago, a lump more than half an inch in diameter was discovered in one of her breasts. Her doctor scheduled a biopsy.

A prayer group gathered at her home the night before this procedure was to take place. Her friends prayed not that the lump would be benign, but rather, that it would disappear entirely.

Nancy is a member of a denomination that takes the Bible literally. In Matthew 18:19-20, Jesus is reported to have said, "Again, I tell you that if two of you on earth agree about anything you ask for, it will be done for you by my Father in heaven. For where two or three come together in my name, there I am with them."

As you can imagine, it was more than two or three. It was a living room full. The next morning, upon self-examination, the lump in her breast appeared to have vanished. But nonetheless Nancy kept her appointment at the hospital where her doctor conducted a thorough examination.

The lump indeed was gone. Not a trace could be found, and the bewildered doctor sent her home.

How could a solid lump of tissue disappear? It melted away due to the potent combination of belief and expectation. We indeed create our own reality.

Jesus also said, "Therefore I tell you, whatever you ask for in prayer, believe that you have received it, and it will be yours." (Mark 11:24) Notice the tense change in this verse. Jesus is saying to believe that you already have what you ask for and it will be given to you in the future. Jesus apparently knew that thoughts are things and that what we believe already exists in the nonphysical realm of spirit as a thought form. Thoughts are things, as we will see, that are ready to materialize on the physical plane.

How are beliefs able to do this? It has to do with the different levels of mind. You might call them lower and higher, or subjective and objective. What differentiates the higher from the lower is the recognition of self. Microbes, plants, worms, and fish possess the lower kind only. They are unaware of self. Even higher animals such as squirrels and other animals of the forest are likely totally unaware of self. This is indicated by the fact that an antelope, for example, does not seem to become angry with a lion when the lion kills and eats one of it's young. Once the lion is out of sight, the antelope simply resumes going about its business of grazing.

Perhaps some animals, dogs and other pets and perhaps dolphins, elephants and whales, have some level of self-awareness. I once had a dachshund that would let me know his displeasure by pooping on the rug when I left him alone for what he apparently considered too long a time. Certainly all humans, even small children, are self aware, and so it appears that the higher variety of self-aware thought is possessed in progressively larger amounts as if ascending a scale. At the present stage of evolution on Earth, humans possess the top level of consciousness, and within each of us are all the other levels down to the subjective, non-dual ground-of-being mind.

Here are the levels of mind as related to me by a professor at the College of Metaphysics in Windyville, Missouri:

- An Individual's Conscious Mind
- An Individual's Unconscious Mind, accumulated during the current life
- An Individual's Subconscious Mind, accumulated during all his or her incarnations
- The Collective Subconscious Mind of humankind, containing the archetypes and what is sometimes called the Akashic Records
- The Subjective, Non-Dual Ground-of-Being Mind of the Creator

Level Five, the ground of being subjective mind, is the organizing intelligence or mind present everywhere that, among other things, supports and controls the mechanics of life in every species and in every individual. It causes plants to grow toward the sun and to push roots into the soil. It causes hearts to beat and lungs to take in air. It controls all of the so-called involuntary functions of the body. And the fact is, it controls a lot more, including all physical and metaphysical laws.

Level Two, an individual's unconscious mind, contains the beliefs that have been established in this life, and like all levels after the conscious mind, the unconscious mind is subjective, meaning it cannot think outside of itself. This is why your beliefs create your reality. Your unconscious subjective mind determines your circumstances and your reality because it blends into and is part of the mind we all share and because of this influences events either favorably or unfavorably based on your beliefs. In addition, your beliefs —whether conscious or unconscious — influence the decisions and the choices you make.

Years ago, I read a series of lectures given in the early twentieth century in Scotland by a man named Thomas Troward (1847-1916) that made a lot of sense. He said the conscious mind has power over the unconscious subjective mind, and the subjective mind creates your reality. I discovered the truth of this firsthand in college when I learned to hypnotize others. I would put a willing classmate into a trance and tell him he was a chicken or a dog. Much to the amusement of my audience, he would then act accordingly.

Hypnotism works because the hypnotist bypasses his subject's conscious mind and speaks directly to the subject's subjective mind. Because of this, a subject's conscious, objective mind is unable to question or disregard the hypnotist's directive. Of course, once the subject emerges from the hypnotic trance, his or her objective mind will take over and will be able to nullify the hypnotist's directive. Nevertheless, while the subject remains in trance, the subject's subjective mind has no choice but to bring into reality what the hypnotist instructs it to do.

The Role of Feelings in Changing Beliefs

If you want to change a belief buried in your unconscious mind, it's important to realize that how you feel about the belief, or you sense of "knowing at a gut level" whether or not it is true, is as important as facts and logic are when it comes to convincing the subjective mind to discard it. So, if you have been brought up to believe and feel, for example, that you are a victim and will never amount to anything, or that people in your family are destined to be overweight, you actually will be a victim and never amount to anything, and you will also be overweight—until, that is, those beliefs change and your subjective mind is reprogrammed.

As stated, the subjective mind cannot step outside of itself and take an objective look. As such, it is capable only of deductive reasoning, which is the kind that progresses from a cause (what is programmed into it) forward to its ultimate end. Having the mind of a deer, a rabbit or a squirrel, it does not stop to question or analyze. This is the same reasoning a criminal might use in committing a crime. He may walk into a room, see a man counting his money, and think: "I need money, so I will take his. Since the man is protecting the money, I will get rid of him. I'll shoot him. He'll drop to the floor. I will then take the money and run. I'll leave by the window." The subjective mind is non-dual. Right and wrong, good and bad, are never considered—only how to get to the end result.

On the other hand, the conscious mind, being objective and self-aware, can step outside. It can reason both deductively and inductively. To reason inductively is to move backward from result to cause. A police detective, for example, would arrive at the crime scene and begin reasoning backward in an attempt to tell how the crime was committed, and who might have done it.

So, if you have a victim mentality, your subjective mind will filter out all sorts of opportunities that come your way because it determines what you notice and are attracted to out of the literally millions of things you are exposed to each day, and it is determined to make your beliefs come true. Therefore, if your subjective mind is convinced you are a victim, and nothing you do can change that, it will dismiss out of hand all sorts of opportunities that might lead to a better life if you would only notice and take advantage of them.

It follows that if you want to change your life, you must change your beliefs, and this may not be easy. Repetition of the new belief you want to adopt will help, but it may not be enough by itself because, as mentioned above, you have to *feel* the belief you want to adopt is true.

Toward Higher States of Consciousness

There have always been a few people who believe we are sparks of the Divine that have evolved on Earth because of an innate desire to become perfectly balanced in terms of love and wisdom until we finally merge back into the Source at the end of our journey in the physical plane of existence. If this is true, it means that to move ahead we must find the "distortions" within us—what I think of has harmful beliefs or negative thought structures. Some would say they are "shadows." Whatever term you prefer, you must purge them from your unconscious mind in order to advance.

Since the unconscious, subjective mind does not know what are good beliefs and what are harmful beliefs, and you may not even be aware they are buried there, the first step is to identify the beliefs you need to change. Beliefs are points of view you have about yourself and the world, and points of view can be changed. They are ideas we think about often, and once we have thought frequently enough about one, the unconscious mind assumes it must be important to your survival as the person you think yourself and wish to be. So, the mind condenses it into a belief, once an idea has become a belief, it exists outside of your conscious awareness.

Let's say because of how you were raised you have a belief you are unworthy of love. If someone asked you if you think you are unworthy of love, you likely would say "No, of course not." You might even be insulted that the individual had the nerve to ask you that.

Unfortunately, you cannot simply look into your conscious mind to discover your beliefs. The way to go about it is to observe your own behavior and life situation because how you behave and where you are today are the results of your unconscious beliefs and opinions. As already discussed, in addition to influencing how you react and your choices, your unconscious mind blends with the universal subconscious mind, causing it to bring into your life what you unconsciously believe about yourself and the world outside you.

Let me interject here that a frequent misconception is that your thoughts create your reality. This is not so because thoughts occur only in the conscious mind, and the unconscious mind is the instrument that creates your reality. Only when a thought is given enough significance to create a belief does the thought gain power. Therefore, a thought you consider to be insignificant or untrue is powerless. The truth is, you give all thoughts their meaning, or the lack thereof. As has been said, a subjective mind does not judge whether something is right or wrong, good or evil. You arrived on this planet a blank canvas on which you can paint the life you want, so why not take advantage of that and do so?

To begin, it is important to understand that your ego is not you and does not have your best interests at heart. The ego's primary goal is its own survival. It is fully aware of your personal reality at all times and constantly judges whether your reality is in sync with your beliefs. It draws upon them to create thoughts and impulses that attract your attention, thereby seeking to reinforce and uphold those beliefs. Therefore, unless you discover what your unconscious beliefs are, the ego will always be in charge, directing your life.

You can determine the beliefs that govern your life by noticing what repeatedly happens in your life. For example, are you a man or a woman who always seems to attract a member of the opposite sex who ends up abusing you? If so, you must have an unconscious belief you are unworthy and deserve abuse. What are other things that consistently go wrong? A buried belief is the reason.

Something else you can do is take note of anything that sets you off or "triggers" you because that is a result of one of your core beliefs. Here's a simple example: suppose your father was critical of you and frequently criticized you with the result as you grew up you felt that nothing you did was ever good enough. Now let's say in your current job you have a male boss older than you, and any time he gives you criticism—even though it may be constructive and meant to be helpful—you immediately feel a sense of fear and anxiety. You have just experienced a trigger because you were conditioned by your father from childhood to believe you are incapable of success. The same process is playing out in obvious and subtle ways in every aspect of your life.

If you want to improve your life and move forward in your quest to live every day in the kingdom of heaven on Earth, you need to notice any time you react to a situation. Then think about your reaction and drill down until you identify the core negative belief that brought it about. Once you have put your finger on it, you can begin the process of changing it to what you want to believe about yourself. Once the belief has been expunged, or replaced with one that's positive, your life will change for the better. Some say the energy centers of our body develop blockages based upon such thoughts and perceptions. If one is lacking in some form of self-love or wisdom, that distorted energy will manifest in one or more of the energy centers. In order to unblock these energy centers to become balanced, we must heal the distortions within us.

I'm aware of two ways this can be done, which are known as the "feminine" approach and the "masculine" approach, the feminine being the positive and masculine the negative polarity — the positive being love and the negative being wisdom. This does not mean that love is good and wisdom is evil. Both polarities are equally valid expressions of the Creator, and that achieving the balance between love and wisdom within the self is crucial for spiritual evolution. Both approaches, while different, can be effective. The feminine heals through transmutation, and the masculine heals through recognition. Which one you favor is up to you.

The Feminine Approach to Balancing

The feminine approach to balancing is accomplished through feeling, thereby purging the unwanted thought form through love. It involves going to the root of the negative emotion, feeling it completely, and allowing it to express itself. Rather than meeting it with resistance, the key is to meet it with love and acceptance, and then, although it may be painful, review and to an extent relive the experience that caused it.

The feminine approach is much more painful and intense than the masculine approach, but it is also much more powerful and immediate. A single healing session has the potential to purify an old wound that has been festering for decades. It takes time, practice, and courage to develop the skill of locating repressed emotions and the memories that are their causes so that you can face them and feel them, but the power of the distorted beliefs and points of view they brought about will be healed quickly as a result.

The Masculine Approach to Balancing

Attaining wisdom and understanding is the masculine approach to healing. Illusions are banished by perceiving that that is simply what they are—illusions. Unlike the feminine, which seeks to heal repressed energy by feeling it out of existence, the masculine approach seeks to defuse and disperse the energy out of existence. It is not as immediate and powerful as the feminine approach, but it is less painful and intense. It is the one I personally prefer, and the one that works best for me. What is required is a permanent shift in perception or attitude, which over time will drain a debilitating thought form of its power.

Here is how I suggest you begin. Step back and observe your own behavior. Once you become aware what is going on, and you are conscious of how you are reacting in different situations, you will have the power to change. To employ this technique successfully, my advice is to put all your energy and passion into your desire for change. You must want the new belief to be true with your entire being. A fraction of a second exists between the moment something happens and your "triggered" reaction. Stop yourself at that instant. Then change what you think and how you react to conform to your new beliefs—even if at first this feels a little awkward. This will take energy away from the old beliefs and direct it onto the new ones, and it won't be long before you start to feel the truth of your new beliefs and comfortable being your new self.

This is how you change beliefs using the masculine approach: you see them for what they are and *want* them to be. Changing beliefs using this technique takes effort because the unconscious mind needs to see proof it is safe to let go of something that has always been seen as beneficial to your survival. You can do this by constantly and consistently presenting your unconscious mind with the truth and by putting some a effort behind it. By acting as though your new way of reacting is who you are now, your unconscious mind will get the message, and eventually, the desired action will feel natural and come naturally.

Let's get into this a little more deeply. Some people think that they cannot change their beliefs because they cannot get themselves to feel the desired belief is actually true. Even though intellectually and logically they may see an old belief as false, it still feels true, and so they think they are powerless to change. This is because beliefs lead to points of view that you possess, and it takes conscious effort to change a point of view. This is likely why you cannot *feel* what you would like to feel about the new belief you want to adopt. The old points of view are still there at the unconscious level, hanging on, preventing you from releasing the old belief. To let one go, you must admit to yourself, and perhaps even to others you have had conversations with about whatever it is, that you have been wrong—you have been guilty of an error in judgment. In other words, you must identify the points of view and opinions a belief has created and adopt new points of view based on the new belief—thereby replacing the old.

I am living proof that if you really want to, you can change your points of view, and therefore your beliefs through wisdom, knowledge, and your fervent desire to live the truth. As a young man, I was an agnostic bordering on atheist and a confirmed Scientific Materialist. I thought that when you died, that was it, so why not seek pleasure as your number one goal in life. Not so now by any stretch of the imagination. Have you ever seen *Animal House?* That was me back then.

If this approach doesn't work for you at first, it is because some part of you still isn't completely sure that balance and total empowerment is really what you want. In order to change, you must lose all interest in your old beliefs and the old stories that created them. Think of yourself as the captain of a ship, and you have turned the ship in the direction you want to go. The wake is your past—it's behind you. Leave it there—forget about it. It's gone and will dissipate and dissolve into the ocean.

The truth is, you will never break free from the grip of a belief and point of view until you let it go and forgive whoever and whatever brought it about. That's right—forgive and forget. Uncle Charlie molested you and that's why you fear sex and despise men? Uncle Charlie was a pathetic, dirty old man nobody loved, who is worthy of pity. Forgive him.

Mom said you were lazy and good for nothing? She was angry, she was wrong, and her father was a loser who drank himself into the grave. Forgive her. Holding on to bitterness isn't hurting Uncle Charlie or your mom. It is only holding you back and making you miserable. As soon as you desire empowerment more than anything—even more than revenge or sympathy—as soon as you truly make the effort, cultivate the desire, and jettison old baggage, you will be on your way. Then nothing can stop you. Claim it whether or not it feels true right now. Claim it because you want it to be your reality, and you want to be totally free.

When something in you starts to resonate with your new belief, you will have begun the process of implanting it in your unconscious mind. You must send a feeling-based message to that part of you. By claiming it because you truly want it, that is what you will be able to do.

Chapter Fourteen: Clean Out Your Attic

Give this some thought. As mentioned earlier, you have been around and evolving for a long time—all the way back to the first single-cell creatures that formed in the primordial sea—perhaps even before that if Edgar Cayce's was correct that human souls were with God at the outset. Perhaps that's true, but at the very least, you are the product of evolution that took place over a mind-boggling 3.77 billion years. Other hominoids that evolved along the way branched off onto dead-end paths or developed into chimpanzees or gorillas and such. Some, like the Neanderthals, made it pretty far along the evolutionary path, but eventually could no longer hack it and became extinct when your ancestors, Homo sapiens, came along and took over their territory. But you kept going and going like the Energizer Bunny. You continued evolving until you eventually arrived at the very top of the food chain. There can be no doubt about it at all. You are a member of a very exclusive club—one among the most gifted and highly intelligent creatures that has ever lived. You are the pinnacle of life on earth, and you are now ready to make the leap into the kingdom of heaven.

You can do this because your mind is fantastic. Scientists say we humans typically use only a portion of its capacity. It is the most important tool you have—an amazing tool that is very much like a garden. You can cultivate it, pull out the weeds, water it, plant the right seeds, and allow them to grow. Or you can neglect it, and let it run wild. Either way, cultivated or not, it must and it will bring forth whatever is allowed to grow in it. There may be ideas and beliefs that were planted in your mind while you were going up that are doing you no good. They are weeds that need to be pulled out and cast aside. Plant good, helpful ideas and beliefs in their place. If good seeds are not planted in your mind and allowed to flourish, destructive weeds will take over and will continue producing more of their kind. Just as a gardener or farmer cultivates his plot of land, weeding it, and growing flowers and the fruits and the vegetables he or she wants on the dinner table, so may a person tend his or her mind, weeding out the useless and destructive thoughts and cultivating only those that have the promise of bearing delicious fruit. If such cultivation does not take place, if discipline is not exercised, the result will not be good because what's in your mind will eventually be what's in your world.

As was discussed, over time the outer conditions of a person's life always come to be in tune with his or her inner state. By the process of planting and cultivating positive, constructive thoughts, you will sooner or later discover that you are the master gardener of your mind—the director of your life; captain of your ship of fate. You will also come to understand that your thoughts and beliefs shape your character, which also creates your circumstances. Ultimately, what's in your mind is your destiny. In Chapter Eight I mentioned a book by a man named James Allen [1864-1912] that I highly recommend called, *As a Man Thinketh.* It's a short book that's worth reading because it vividly illustrates that each man and each woman creates his or her personal reality with their thoughts and beliefs.

Something else to know along this line is that the unconscious mind does not understand, or perhaps simply doesn't hear the words "no" and "not." Suppose, for example, you're a tennis player. You're in a big match, it's close, and you are now in a tiebreaker. The next point could decide the match. The point has come for your opponent to serve. As you pass by him at the net changing ends, you say, "You're playing great today, Henry. Don't blow it. This is a big point coming up. Whatever you do, do not double fault."

You've started Henry worrying, and on top of that, his unconscious mind doesn't hear or understand the word "not." All it hears is "do double fault," and it takes that as a directive. Try as he might to do otherwise, Henry will double fault.

Actually, I advise you not to play such a dirty trick. As the saying goes, "What goes around, comes around," and you don't want that sort of negative behavior coming back at you. More will be written about this. The important thing to remember is that self-talk and coaching should always be framed in a positive way.

Think Positive and Rid Yourself of Fear

Let's dig into the issue of fear because fears are beliefs and feelings, and beliefs and feelings are what create your reality.

To learn what you fear, as suggested in the previous chapter, tune into your moment-to-moment stream of consciousness and observe what makes you worried, anxious, resentful, uptight, afraid, angry, and so on. Step outside yourself and identify unsettled emotions, tugs and urges that have become part of your programming. Slow down and consider what triggered a negative emotion. Did your temper flare? Why? Why was it so important for things to go a certain way? If you trace what you felt back to its cause, you might come to a particular variety of fear, and it's been said that only two fears are instinctive: the fear of falling and loud noises. Other fears were acquired, and whatever was acquired can be disposed of.

According to some experts, the fears that hold people back can be grouped under one of six headings:

> the fear of poverty (or failure),
> the fear of criticism,
> the fear of ill health,
> the fear of the loss of love,
> the fear of old age,
> and the fear of death.

I've listed the fear of poverty (failure) first because in many ways it can be the most debilitating. It is self-fulfilling in that traits develop that bring it about. For example, are you a procrastinator? An underlying fear of failure is probably the root cause and can be counted upon to produce the result you fear.

Are you overly cautious? Do you see the negative side of every circumstance or stall for the "right time" before taking action? Do you worry (that things will not work out), have doubts (generally expressed by excuses or apologies about why one probably won't be able to perform), suffer from indecision (which leads to someone else, or circumstances, making the decision for you)?

Are you indifferent? This generally manifests as laziness or a lack of initiative, enthusiasm or self-control.

Step back and listen for internal voices that say "can't" or "don't" or "won't" or "too risky" or "why bother?"

How do you get rid of them? Shoo them away.

Whether you are the president of a company, or a bum on Skid Row, the only thing over which you have absolute control is your thoughts.

You may say, I can't control what thoughts pop into my head. True. You may not control what thoughts arise, but you can decide whether to discard one or to keep it. You can decide that it is counterproductive and throw it away, or you can turn it over and over in your mind, nurture it and let it grow. Whatever thoughts you keep will expand and eventually manifest themselves.

Beginning now, each time you catch yourself with a negative thought, a thought that says "you can't," "it's not possible," "maybe someone else but not me," get rid of it. Shoo it away.

But you say, "I'm poor, I'm not a good student, I'm not a good salesperson, I'm in the lower third of productivity."

That's your ego talking. You are what you are because of your unconscious beliefs. You want the best for yourself, but your unconscious ego-mind is holding you back because of the way it was programmed.

If what I've been writing about on this page is a serious problem for you, follow the advice given in the last chapter, and go out and buy some self-help tapes that will plant positive thoughts in your mind in place of the negative ones. Play them to and from work and before you go to sleep at night. Use self-hypnosis tapes. Play them over and over for at least a month. Get all that junk out of your head, and replace it with thoughts that are positive.

What about the other fears? They're to be discarded in the same manner. If you suffer from fear of criticism, for example, it probably came about as a result of a parent or sibling who constantly tore you down to build himself up. You'll know this is a problem if you are overly worried about what others might think, if you lack poise, are self-consciousness or extravagant. (Why extravagant? Because of the voice which says you need to keep up with the Joneses.) You must rid yourself of inner voices that tell you to think even twice about what others will say. Take advantage of that fraction of a second between stimulus and response, stop to remember this, and let it sink in. That's how you can change—how to eliminate destructive fears and beliefs.

Let's think for a minute about the fear of criticism. There have been places and times in history when what others thought was worth worrying about. My great, great, great, great, great, great, great grandmother, Suzanna Martin, for example, was accused of being a witch, falsely convicted, and hanged in Salem, Massachusetts, in 1692. She was an old lady. Probably, she looked like a witch. But her downfall was the stir she caused after her husband died. She was able to run the farm successfully without a man around. Think of the talk. Such a thing wasn't possible, or so they believed, without the use of witchcraft.

The opinions of Suzanna Martin's neighbors mattered a great deal. They led to an unpleasant and untimely death.

What about today?

In Iran, China, Russia, or North Korea one might have to watch out what neighbors think or what the "virtue police" hear, but this simply is no longer a valid concern in developed, democratic countries. What others think or don't think of you or anyone else is their problem. Yet worrying about what they think can cause a great deal of misery, create karma that will have to be worked out, and cause interference between your conscious and your subconscious minds that blocks the channel of communication.

What about the fear of ill health?

To rid yourself of this, it should be enough to know that what you worry and think about is eventually what happens. Ever noticed that it's the people who talk about illness, worry about illness, are preoccupied with this or that possible illness, think they feel a pain here or there or were exposed to some germ, who are precisely the people who stay sick most of the time? The power of suggestion is at work.

How about the fear of the loss of love? This one manifests in the form of jealousy and is self-fulfilling like the others. The person you try so hard to hang onto feels smothered, with the result that you end up pushing that person away. Try being yourself. Give them love, but give them room. If they leave you, they would have done so anyway. You can now move on to a truly meaningful relationship.

Next is the fear of old age. This is closely connected to the fear of ill health and the fear of poverty because these are the conditions a person really is concerned about deep down. The power of suggestion is hard at work here, too. If you think you're too old to do this or that, you will indeed be too old.

Consider this. My children are the same flesh and blood as my wife and me. I saw them being born, still connected by umbilical cords. I clipped the cord of one of them myself. My wife was thirty-six at the time our youngest was born. I was fifty-four. Yet the cells in my body, and in my wife's body, and in my son's body all were the most recent in an unbroken chain of cell division that goes back to the first life on earth. All the cells—my wife's, my son's, and mine—are at the end of a chain that is precisely the same age: billions of years. As the physic Egar Cayce often said in trance, "Spirit is the life, mind is the builder. The physical is the result." Those telomeres get shorter and shorter because you think that you should look and feel older as the years go by. The physical body is the overcoat of the mental body. It gets old and decrepit because a person expects it to. It gets older and decrepit because a person stops learning, growing, and playing a role in the evolution of humankind.

When you've learned all you can from this life, the time will come for you to check out. And check out is what you will. No one says you have to be old.

Now we've come to that final bugaboo, the fear of death. As you now have seen, there's nothing to fear except having been fearful in this life. Consider the millions who have had near-death experiences and are no longer afraid to die. They're convinced they'll be greeted by their guides as well as by loved ones who have gone before. They look forward to being bathed once again in the all-encompassing light, which many have described as total, unconditional love. Most do not expect to experience pain. It has been reported by many that the spirit exits the body the instant it looks as though death is inevitable.

Only a handful who have had hellish experiences worry about what they may encounter in the nonphysical world. These folks need to know what you know. Each of us creates his own reality. We experience what we expect to experience, what we think we deserve. In the physical world, this takes time. In the nonphysical world of spirit, which is the medium of the mind, we instantly create our reality, just as we do in dreams. If we expect Hell, the Hell we believe we deserve is the Hell we will get. If we expect Heaven, our vision of Heaven is what we will have.

Anyone who has ever had a lucid dream will understand what I mean. Such a dream is one in which a person realizes he's dreaming. I've had many and I look forward to them because it's more fun than Disney World. As soon as you're aware you're dreaming, you can begin to compose the dream, determine the players, the surroundings, the action. Want to fly over the Grand Canyon? All you have to do is "think" this. Fly over is what you will do, no airplane required. Like anything it takes practice, but I've gotten so I can swoop and turn and loop the loop.

Want to attend a cocktail party populated by Hollywood stars? You'll be there with Robert DeNiro or Julia Roberts. These characters will, of course, be your own thought projections.

You are a dreamer in the Creator's big dream of life, and you can make your waking dream lucid as well. Until now, you may have thought you were at the mercy of conditions outside yourself, that you've either been lucky or unlucky, that chance has brought you where you are. This isn't true. You've brought yourself to this spot, either consciously or unconsciously. If this is not where you want to be, you've arrived because your unconscious mind has been programmed incorrectly, and you are totally out of touch with your Higher Self. Perhaps you hear snippets from it every now and then but ignore what it's trying to say because of other voices which beat it back with "can't," "don't," "shouldn't," "too risky." These are the words of your ego. Your Higher Self wants you to evolve and to enter the kingdom.

Until you started reading this book, you may have thought you were at the mercy of conditions outside yourself, that you have either been lucky or unlucky, and that chance has brought you where you are today. Not so. You brought yourself to this place, and you did so unconsciously. If this is not where you want to be, you will have to change your programming, which likely took place when you were a child.

The Power of Positive Thinking

I suspect you have heard about "The Power of Positive Thinking," that positive thoughts are much more likely to produce good results than negative thoughts. I'm reminded of *The Little Engine That Could,* an American fairy tale published numerous times in illustrated children's books and movies since its original debut in 1930. The Little Engine was a railroad locomotive that was tasked with pulling a long, heavy train—one that seemed much too large for it—up and over a mountain. But even so, the Little Engine was determined and kept telling itself over and over, "I think I can, I think I can." It was a struggle, but the Little Engine persevered and finally succeeded.

It's a good story and a valuable one to teach young children the benefits of optimism and hard work. The problem is, many of us today were not taught that lesson as children, and in fact, feelings of frustration, discontent, and dissatisfaction were ways of solving problems that many of us "learned" as infants. For example, if a baby is hungry, he or she expresses discontent by crying. Lo and behold, a warm and tender hand appears magically out of nowhere and brings a bottle of milk. Later on, if the baby is uncomfortable, again, he or she will again express dissatisfaction, and the same warm, comforting hands magically appear and solve the problem. That's fine for babies but, unfortunately, many children continue to get their way and have their problems solved by indulgent parents merely by continuing to express their feelings of frustration when things don't work the way they want. All they have to do is feel frustrated and dissatisfied, express their dissatisfaction, and the problem will be solved. Sometimes what have become known as "helicopter parents" continue to cater to their children in this way all the way through high school, college, and beyond.

This way of life "works" for infants, and for some children. But it does not work in adult life when a person is out in the world on his or her own. Yet many continue to expect, perhaps unconsciously, that it will work. They seem to think that by feeling discontented and expressing their grievances—if only they feel put upon enough—life, or someone will take pity on them, rush to their aid and solve their problems. Let me assure you that 99.99 percent of the time that is not going to happen. It is my advice that you take responsibility for every aspect of your life.

Imagine, for example, you land an entry-level job as a management trainee in a big corporation. With you in training are several other bright young men and women fresh out of business school. Imagine the way things work in this company is often not to your liking. Management trainees, for example, are relegated to cubicles with five-foot-high walls affording little or no privacy, while the senior staff all have corner offices with large windows and spectacular views of the East River. You spend a good deal of time grumbling to yourself and to others about this injustice, subconsciously believing that will get you out of that cubicle and into a corner suite. Your fellow trainees, on the other hand, spend their time making positive suggestions and anticipating and providing for the needs of customers as well as for fellow workers higher up on the corporate ladder. Whom do you suppose is most likely to be first to break out of his or her cubicle? The one who constantly complained? Or the one that consistently delivered the goods?

Don't you feel a twinge inside that intuitively "knows" the positive attitude, the attitude of service to others, will inevitably win the day? That "twinge" is a message from something inside you that knows the correct answer called "intuition."

If you have been ignoring that feeling when it comes, now is the time for you to begin recognizing such messages. They have a light and airy feeling to them, even though they may seem to run counter to egocentric notions, such as, "The first order of business is to look out for number one." That egocentric notion may work in the short term, but in the long term, it is bad advice. The fact is that it's always best to under-promise and over-deliver to customers and bosses—as well as to anyone else for that matter. By over-delivering, your reputation grows as you create positive vibes and positive opinions of you by those with whom you come in contact. A reputation that you are someone who can be counted on can only lead to good outcomes and opportunities for you in the long run.

Let's consider for a moment why some people may spend their valuable time on earth grumbling and complaining away opportunities to get ahead. It's often because they have felt frustrated and defeated for so long—ever since they were babies in a crib and while growing up with indulgent parents—that those feelings have become ingrained. Their minds are in a kind of holding pattern, and it's never occurred to them to step outside of themselves in order to get in touch with intuition that would tell them, if they would only listen, that grumbling and complaining are counterproductive and accomplish nothing. Until they wise up, they will continue—to their own detriment—to radiate those feelings, and as night follows day, their discontent will lead to failure.

No matter what your mindset, if you want to change it, it's important to realize, as has been discussed, that beliefs and feelings are intertwined. It might be said that feelings are the soil in which thoughts and ideas grow. If you are habitually grumpy and in a bad mood, you need to lighten up and begin seeing the glass half full. Moreover, when you begin working toward a goal, try thinking how you will feel when you reach it—and then actually make yourself feel that way. I'm serious. Conjure up the feeling of "Success!" The thrill of accomplishment will communicate the belief to your unconscious mind that it's inevitable you are going to achieve what you have set out to accomplish. The feeling creates the belief, and the belief creates the feeling. A mental model of success will be etched into your unconscious, and that the desired outcome will surely come about.

Let's say you are pursuing a challenge and fervently want to accomplish it. Assuming you have the education, the knowledge, and the qualifications required to reach your goal, and assuming you feel strongly about it at an emotional level, you will almost certainly realize success. This will happen because your unconscious mind, which is connected to the universal subconscious and all other minds, will go to work and act like a magnet, drawing to you what you need. The greater your desire, the more powerfully your unconscious mind will strive to produce results.

In summary, belief and emotions are the keys. It's important to feel the joy of having accomplished what you set out to accomplish before it actually happens. This will convince your subconscious the goal has already been reached and the universal mind will cause it to be reached as a result.

Be Likable and Appealing to Others

Leaving psychological suffering behind will require effort and work, and that means things will be easier if you have help along the way. The most likely source of that help will be friends, partners, and mentors. Obviously, the going will be easier and you will attract more help if people like you and want to work with you. Therefore, it should go without saying that it's important to be someone others want to be around—someone people would like and want as a friend. That means you need to be someone who "talks the talk," and "walks the walk." Perhaps you know a person who does the opposite. If not, you are likely to come across someone like that in your business dealings, so be prepared and never, ever be one of them. In public such people talk openly—some even brag and boast—about the importance of having integrity and doing the right thing. But in private it's a different story. They bad mouth people and do things that aren't consistent with the honest-John public persona they hope to project. People quickly see through these phonies. As the old saying goes, "Say what you mean, and mean what you say," and people will respect you for doing so.

Obey the Laws of Physics

If you are a materialist and think matter is all that exists—that there is no God and nothing spiritual—you might come to the conclusion you can do whatever you want, harm whomever you want, and never have to suffer any consequences. But that is not how things work. I agree it may work for a while, but eventually you'll get back what you gave out because, just has there are laws of physics, there are laws of metaphysics. People must obey them, and nations must as well. Take Japan and Germany in World War II as examples. Both countries had astonishing victories in the beginning. Each country benefited from a national zeitgeist that they were invincible. But they ended up being crushed because the atrocities they committed came back upon them with a vengeance.

Always Keep Your Life in Balance

You are probably familiar with the ancient Chinese symbol composed of a white "yin" interlocking a black "yang" that represents the dual nature of things. It symbolizes that we live in a world that is composed of opposites: Up, down, black, white, good and evil. Without the tension opposites create, nothing would or could exist—everything would fall apart. Follow the advice of this book and enter the kingdom but do not allow complacency to set in. Always seek new challenges, realizing that without one, self-destruction may result. Always strive to continue growing.

It can also be comforting to know there can be no growth without at least some discontent. Deep within, you know what is best for you. There is an urge built into you that pushes you to strive for growth, and for most of us, growth will not continue without some agitation and discontent. So study your dissatisfactions. They will tell you what you are about to leave behind and possibly point you in a new direction. Be willing to be uncomfortable. It is the way to grow.

As you contemplate your future course, it is also important to realize you can only attract that which you feel worthy of. Self-esteem is critical to success. That's why I urge you to get rid of the psychological baggage. The truth is you are not what you have, and you are not what you do. Beneath your fear and negative programming, you are perfect—an enlightened soul, fully self-actualized and a living example of unconditional love. The more you can let go of fears, the higher your self esteem will be, and the more options you will have and more risks you can take. The more you like yourself, the more others will like you, and the more worthy you will feel.

You can have anything you want if you can give up the belief that you cannot have it—assuming what you want does not conflict with someone else's belief. If, for example, you desire a fulfilling, one-to-one relationship, but demand it to be with a particular person, you are not operating in harmony with the universe.

Another example is in the area of accomplishment. You must get the education necessary to create what you want. "Where your attention goes, your energy flows." You attract what you believe you are and that which you concentrate upon. If you are negative, you draw in and experience negativity. If you are loving, you draw in and experience love. You can attract to you only those qualities you possess. So, if you want peace and harmony in your life, you must become peaceful and harmonious.

Something else to understand is that a stronger emotion will always dominate a weaker one. Every idea can be the beginning of a manifestation—although unless you nurture it, think about and develop feelings about the idea, it will not become expressed in reality. It does not matter which idea you consciously favor, even know to be desirable, a stronger emotion will nullify a weaker one, and the strongest emotion will begin to permeate all aspects of your activities. For example, if you are emotionally focused on the sexual desirability of a particular person, you may begin to create circumstances that will increase the likelihood of an eventual sexual union.

It is also important to realize that new information you accept into your mind will destroy previous information of a similar nature. Once a pathway of information has been created in you, a new viewpoint will develop and prevail unless new information comes in to replace and destroy it. Let's say, for example, you fall off and get hurt while horseback riding. That may be the end of your experience with horses because you will have just been programmed negatively about horseback riding. This is why instructors always urge new riders to climb back aboard immediately. You need new, positive input to erase the trauma of the fall.

The mind is engaged in an endless state of growth and reorganization. As a result, it is possible to reprogram yourself. You can do this by using the feminine or masculine techniques described previously, or some combination of the two, and by reinforcing new beliefs and points of view by repeatedly listening to success-meditation recordings and using visualization techniques. If you feel anxiety in crowds, imagine yourself relaxed in a crowd of people. When you fear doing something, and yet have the courage to do it anyway, you will soon do a mental flip-flop and may even become addicted to doing it.

Here is a case in point. Suppose you fear skydiving, or skiing fast almost straight down a steep mountain. If you force yourself to do so anyway, the experience will release endorphins, which are produced by the central nervous system and the pituitary gland and can produce a feeling of euphoria very similar to that produced by opiates. The result can be that you become somewhat addicted to skiing fast down mountains and skydiving.

You have within you everything required to make your earthly incarnation a paradise if you choose to accept that which is your divine birthright. We live in a universe of abundance, although the majority of humans populating our planet appear to view it as a universe of scarcity.

Heed the call. Take the leap. But do not go off half-cocked. Plan it out. Take a full day. Take more than one. Take as many as necessary to develop your plan.

No matter what else you may decide to do, always remember the secret of life. What follows is a short book I wrote a few years ago that will give you more insight into the true nature of reality

Chapter Fifteen: The Discovery That Changes Everything

For more than three centuries humanity has lived under a powerful assumption that the universe is fundamentally mechanical. Matter came first. Consciousness appeared later as a by-product of complex brains. Human beings, according to this view, are biological machines that briefly become aware before disappearing again into the silence of matter. This idea shaped modern science, medicine, education, and culture, but as we have seen throughout this book, the evidence increasingly suggests that this assumption may have the true nature of things backwards.

The emerging picture of reality is very different. Rather than consciousness arising from matter, matter may arise within consciousness. Instead of the brain producing awareness, the brain may function more like a receiver or interface—thus allowing a deeper field of consciousness to interact with the physical world. If true, human beings are not accidental by-products of a blind universe, but rather, we may represent one way the universe is becoming aware of itself.

The Pattern Hidden in the Evidence

Taken individually, many of the phenomena discussed in this book might seem puzzling or controversial:

- Near-death experiences suggest awareness can persist when brain activity is severely impaired.
- Children's memories of past lives challenge the idea that personal identity begins at birth.
- Experiments in parapsychology hint that our minds may extend beyond the boundaries of the body.
- Quantum physics reveals that matter itself is not solid but a dynamic pattern of energy and probability.

Neuroscience continues to confront the mystery that subjective experience—the inner world of awareness—cannot be explained in purely physical terms. Each of these findings points toward the same possibility: Consciousness may not be a late arrival in the universe. It may actually be the foundation of it. Max Planck, the father of quantum theory, reached precisely this conclusion nearly a century ago when he said:

"I regard consciousness as fundamental.
I regard matter as derivative from consciousness."

At the time, few scientists were prepared to follow that idea to its logical conclusion. Today, however, the evidence pointing in that direction is becoming increasingly difficult to ignore.

A Universe Becoming Aware

If consciousness truly is fundamental, then the story of the universe takes on a very different meaning. From the first atoms formed in ancient stars to the emergence of life on Earth, the cosmos has been evolving toward greater complexity. With complexity came nervous systems. With nervous systems came awareness, And with the appearance of human beings came something extraordinary: self-awareness.

Perhaps for the first time in cosmic history, the universe gained the ability to reflect upon itself. Through human consciousness, the universe can ask questions about its own origin. Through human curiosity, it can explore the laws that govern its structure. Through human imagination, it can envision possibilities that do not yet exist. In this sense, the evolution of life may represent the gradual awakening of the cosmos.

Why We Are Here

If the emerging scientific picture is correct, then the ancient question—*Why are we here?*—may have a surprisingly simple answer. We are here to experience. We are here to learn. We are here to participate in and contribute to the unfolding of consciousness.

Every human life adds something to that process. Every experience—joyful or painful—expands the range of what consciousness understands about itself and the universe that it has created and inhabits.

Seen from this perspective, existence is not meaningless. It is exploratory. Life becomes a vast experiment in awareness.

The Future of the Scientific Worldview

History shows that scientific revolutions often begin slowly. New ideas first appear as anomalies—observations that do not fit the existing framework. For a time those anomalies are dismissed or ignored, but eventually they accumulate until the old framework can no longer hold. At that point a new worldview emerges.

Today, evidence from physics, neuroscience, psychology, and consciousness research suggests we may be approaching such a turning point as the mechanistic model of reality that dominated the nineteenth and twentieth centuries more and more displays its limitations. The result may be that a deeper understanding of consciousness will become one of, if not the major defining scientific discoveries of the twenty-first century.

What This Means for You

If consciousness is fundamental, then you are far more than a biological machine. Your awareness is not merely the temporary by-product of neurons firing inside a skull. You are an expression of the same underlying consciousness that gives rise to the universe itself.

This realization has profound implications. It means that creativity, purpose, and meaning are not illusions generated by chemistry. They are expressions of a deeper dimension of reality. It means that the human search for truth is not accidental, but rather, an important way the universe is exploring itself.

The Great Adventure

For thousands of years philosophers, mystics, and spiritual traditions have suggested that consciousness is the ultimate foundation of existence. Science is now beginning to rediscover that possibility. If the evidence presented in this book points in the right direction, then we are living at a remarkable moment in intellectual history. Humanity may be on the verge of a new understanding of reality—one that reconnects science with the deepest questions about life, meaning, and the nature of mind.

The implications of that discovery may be greater than any scientific revolution that came before because it would finally answer the questions that have puzzled humanity for centuries:

Who are we?
Why are we here?

The answers may be both humbling and inspiring. We are the universe becoming aware of itself, and the exploration has only just begun.

Chapter Sixteen: A New Idea That's 300 Years Old

In this final chapter, I want to leave with something more to think about. In the early eighteenth century, an Irish philosopher named George Berkeley [1685-1753] set out to challenge what seemed like the most obvious fact in the world: that physical objects exist independently of our minds. From Berkeley's point of view, this assumption—so natural that few people would ever question it—was not only mistaken but unnecessary. He believed that once we examined our experience carefully, we would discover something surprising:

What we call the physical world is not made of matter at all, but of ideas—ideas perceived by minds, and ultimately sustained by an infinite mind.

Berkeley began with a simple observation. Everything we know about the world comes through experience. We see colors, hear sounds, feel textures, taste flavors, and smell scents. These are the building blocks of what we call reality. Berkeley, however, noticed something subtle.

We never experience "matter" itself. We experience only perceptions—the redness of an apple, the hardness of a table, the warmth of sunlight. These qualities exist only as they are perceived.

Try to imagine an object that exists completely unperceived—no color seen, no texture felt, no sound heard.

Berkeley argued that this is impossible.

The moment we attempt to imagine such a thing, we are already perceiving it in our own mind. The very idea of an object existing without being perceived collapses into contradiction. From this he drew his famous conclusion:

"To be is to be perceived" ***(esse est percipi).***

This did not mean, however, that Berkeley believed the world was an illusion or a dream. On the contrary, he insisted that the world is real—deeply and reliably real. Nevertheless, however, its reality does not consist in being made of matter. It consists in being experienced by minds. When you see a tree, what exists is not a material object independent of all observers. What exists is a coherent set of perceptions: color, shape, texture, position—held together in an orderly way. These perceptions are real, but Berkeley did not believe that there was some additional, unseen "material substance" underlying them.

Of course, Berkeley's detractors raised what seems a reasonable question: If objects exist only as they are perceived, what happens when no human is looking at them? Does the tree disappear when no one is in the forest to see it?

Berkeley's answer was that the continuity and stability of the world are guaranteed because everything is always perceived by an infinite mind.

The mind of God, or what I prefer to refer to as "Source."

Even when no human observer is present, the tree continues

to exist because it is perceived by God. The world does not flicker in and out of existence because it is constantly held in being by a divine awareness.

If true, reality is not a collection of inert objects. It is a living field of perception, sustained by a universal consciousness.

Human beings, in Berkeley's philosophy, are also minds—but finite ones. We perceive the world, but we do not create it. The patterns of our experience—the laws of nature, the regularities of perception—are not invented by us. They are presented to us in a consistent and intelligible way.

Berkeley believed this order reflects the activity of God. The world, in effect, is a kind of divine language—a structured system of perceptions through which God communicates with finite minds. When we observe nature, we are not discovering an independent material reality. We are interpreting a pattern of ideas that has been arranged for us.

In this framework, what we call "physical objects" are not substances but bundles of ideas. A table, for example, is not a material thing existing beneath perception. It is a stable collection of sensory qualities—its shape, its color, its solidity—coherently organized and consistently experienced. These qualities exist in minds, and the consistency of their arrangement reflects the ongoing activity of the divine mind.

Berkeley's view leads to a striking conclusion about human identity. If the world is composed of ideas in the mind of God, then we ourselves—our perceptions, our thoughts, our experiences—exist within that same field of awareness. We are not separate from reality in the way materialism suggests, as isolated observers inside a physical universe. Instead, we are participants within a universal consciousness.

In a profound sense, each of us can be understood as an idea in the mind of God—not a passive or insignificant idea, but an active center of perception, capable of awareness, understanding, and relationship.

Berkeley's philosophy was radical in his time, and it remains provocative today. It challenges the common assumption that matter is the foundation of reality and that mind emerges from it. Instead, it proposes the reverse:

Mind is fundamental, and what we call matter is a structured appearance within it.

Though his ideas were initially met with skepticism, they have echoed through centuries of philosophical thought. Later thinkers, from idealist philosophers to some interpreters of modern physics, have revisited the possibility that reality is not as solid and independent as it seems. In this sense, Berkeley's vision can be seen not as a rejection of reality, but as a redefinition of it.

The world is not less real than we thought. It is, perhaps, more intimate.

For Berkeley, the universe is not a machine made of inert parts. It is a continuous act of perception, sustained by an infinite mind.

If George Bekeley was correct, we find ourselves within that act—not as accidental byproducts of matter, but as conscious participants in a reality that is, at its deepest level, mental. In the end, his philosophy invites a quiet but profound shift in perspective:

What we take to be a world "out there" may in fact be a world within consciousness itself—a reality in which to exist is to be perceived, and to perceive is to participate in the unfolding awareness of the whole.

# # #

If you enjoyed this book and thought it was worth your time to read, please let others know by going to the book's page on Amazon and writing a review and/or simply rating it.

About The Author

Stephen Hawley Martin the author of more than three-dozen books, including five published novels, half a dozen business management titles, and quite a few self-help books and metaphysical investigations. He is a former principal of the world-renowned advertising agency, The Martin Agency, the firm that created the GEICO Gecko and "Virginia is for lovers." Today, Stephen is editor and publisher of The Oaklea Press. Listed in *Who's Who in America,* and best known as a award-winning author, Steve is the only three-time winner of the *Writer's Digest* Book Award, having won twice for fiction and once for nonfiction. He has also won First Prize for Visionary Fiction from *Independent Publisher,* First Prize for Nonfiction from *USA Book News,* and a Bronze Metal for Visionary fiction from *Readers' Choice Book Reviews.* He is actively looking for ghostwriting projects and other authors' manuscripts to edit and publish. To get in touch with Stephen, visit his website and use the contact form:

www.shmartin.com

Books You May Want to Read

Now that you realize you are an eternal spiritual being having a temporary physical experience you will want to read the sequel. In it, the author descibes what it was like to merge with the Cosmic Mind, and he shares insights he brought back with him that you can use to find joy in this life and bliss in the next.

Paperback ISBN: 979-8479020360

"Spirit is the life, mind is the builder, and the physical is the result." Repeated often in trance by Edgar Cayce, these words describe the formula behind the existence of all that is, including you and your personal reality. If you want to know how to find your purpose and use this formula to create the best life possible, simply read this book.

Paperback: ISBN: 979-8706169121

This book explains the new world view that's rapidly being accepted by individuals on the cutting edge due to assimilation of the results of quantum physics experiments and consciousness research that's been going on since the 1960s at the University of Virginia School of Medicine. One implication of this research is that we humans are eternal, nonphysical beings having temporary physical experiences.

Paperback: ISBN: 979-8291825013

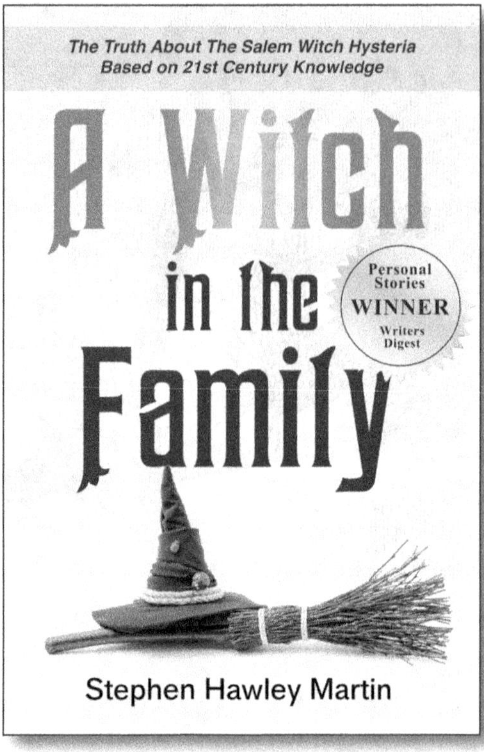

Nineteen were hanged, including the author's seven-times-great grandmother, and one was crushed to death. Were their accusers lying as indicated in Arthur Miller's play, "The Crucible?" Maybe not. This book is a riveting account of a real-life murder mystery. If you'd like to know what really happened in 1692 Salem, don't miss this book.

PB: ISBN-13 : 979-8849635491

In this romantic suspense thriller, Rebecca wants to save the beautiful plantation home where she grew up, but to do so she must find her mother. If only she could remember what happened in the basement of the old house in Baltimore long ago. She must find out what happened there, she must!

Paperback: ISBN-10: 1535580879

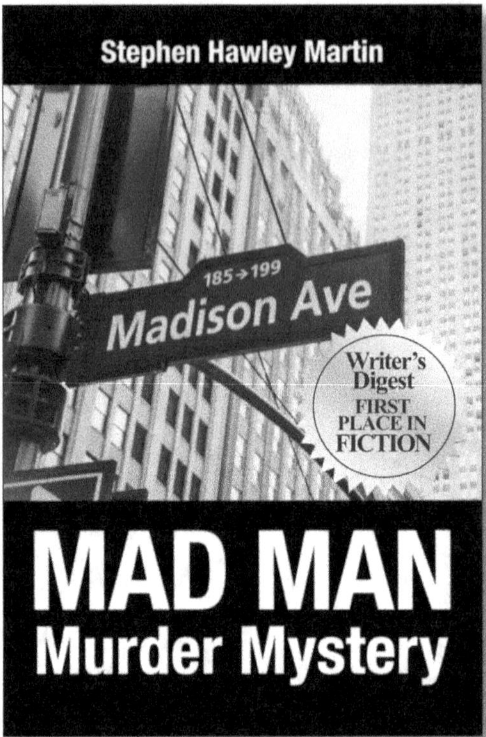

This whodunit set in an ad agency won First Prize for Fiction from *Writer's Digest* magazine. According to Mike Chapman, Editor-in-Chief of *ADWEEK* magazine, this novel is "A thrilling and evocative read. Masterful attention to detail brings the ad agency world to life and delivers a gripping whodunit." Get ready. You won't be able to put it down.

Paperback: ISBN 979-8282125313

Historical fiction at its best, based on an actual catastrophic event, this fast-paced novel won First Prize for Fiction from *Writer's Digest* and First Place for Visionary Fiction from *Independent Publisher* for good reason: It's very hard to put down. You'll be riveted as Claire flies to the island of Martinique to solve a mystery and soon realizes she's being stalked by a drug lord.

ISBN: 979-8591416515

www.ingramcontent.com/pod-product-compliance
Lightning Source LLC
LaVergne TN
LVHW022035200926
848481LV00003B/696

* 9 7 9 8 2 9 5 7 3 5 9 6 7 *